# FINDING BETHLEHEM

A Global Journey Through the
Mepkin Abbey Crèche Festival

# FINDING BETHLEHEM

## A Global Journey Through the Mepkin Abbey Crèche Festival

MEPKIN
ABBEY

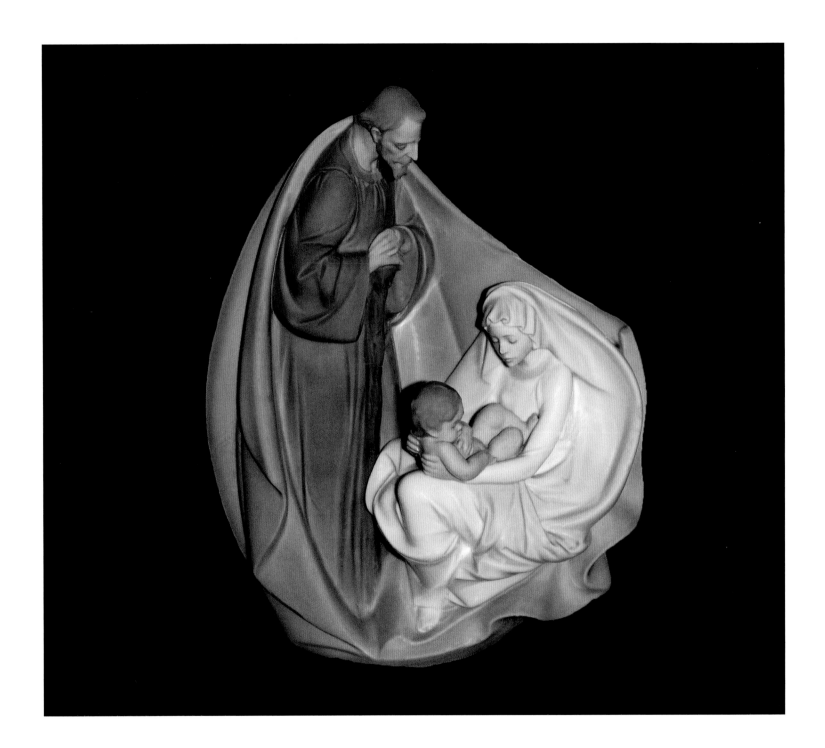

# Luke 2: 1-20

1 In those days a decree went out from Emperor Augustus that all the world should be registered.

2 This was the first registration and was taken while Quirinius was governor of Syria.

3 All went to their own towns to be registered.

4 Joseph also went from the town of Nazareth in Galilee to Judea, to the city of David called Bethlehem, because he was descended from the house and family of David.

5 He went to be registered with Mary, to whom he was engaged and who was expecting a child.

6 While they were there, the time came for her to deliver her child.

7 And she gave birth to her firstborn son and wrapped him in bands of cloth, and laid him in a manger, because there was no place for them in the inn.

8 In that region there were shepherds living in the fields, keeping watch over their flock by night.

9 Then an angel of the Lord stood before them, and the glory of the Lord shone around them, and they were terrified.

10 But the angel said to them, "Do not be afraid; for see—I am bringing you good news of great joy for all the people:

11 To you is born this day in the city of David a Savior, who is the Messiah, the Lord.

12 This will be a sign for you: you will find a child wrapped in bands of cloth and lying in a manger."

13 And suddenly there was with the angel a multitude of the heavenly host, praising God and saying,

14 "Glory to God in the highest heaven, and on earth peace among those whom he favors!"

15 When the angels had left them and gone into heaven, the shepherds said to one another, "Let us go now to Bethlehem and see this thing that has taken place, which the Lord has made known to us."

16 So they went with haste and found Mary and Joseph, and the child lying in the manger.

17 When they saw this, they made known what had been told them about this child;

18 and all who heard it were amazed at what the shepherds told them.

19 But Mary treasured all these words and pondered them in her heart.

20 The shepherds returned, glorifying and praising God for all they had heard and seen, as it had been told them.

Crèche is a word coming down to us from the Old French, meaning a manger, a crib, a stall.  Which is to say, a place to lay one's head, to shelter one's dreams, to swaddle, in the darkness, one's newborn spirit.  And that is what happens here in the Mepkin Abbey Crèche Festival.  A place is created, beyond all worlds, where the whole of the world mangers down, in peace.  A space is made for the light of all people—how wide their colors and tongues and imagination—yet all

are mirrored in the few faces here: the mother and child, the kings and peasants, the angels and animals warmed by a cave. When we find our human diversity at home in this story; when we find something divine alive in this simplicity; when we see our true humanity in this earthly humility; then we have touched the power of Christmas. In the crèches of Mepkin is sheltered our deepest hope for the world.

SUSAN HULL WALKER

Gloria in Excelsis Deo!

I n the Gospel according to Luke, it is said that a multitude of heavenly hosts sang Glory to God in the Highest. As a musician, I would really like to have heard that. Something in me always wants to look up at the angels.

FATHER FRANCIS KLINE, O.C.S.O.

Brothers, let us hasten to the Lord's manger crib, but as far as we can let us first prepare ourselves by his grace to approach it. Then, in the company of the angels, with pure heart, a good conscience and unfeigned faith, let us sing to the Lord in the whole of our life and our monastic conversion: Glory to God in the highest and peace to all of good will.

AELRED OF RIEVAULX
*SERMON ON THE NATIVITY*

*This book is dedicated to the memory of Earl Kage, whose vision and generosity contributed so greatly to the Mepkin Abbey Crèche Festival, and to our volunteers, whose dedication and selflessness make this vision a yearly reality.*

# Contents

# The History of Mepkin Abbey

The history of Mepkin Abbey weaves an amazing story throughout both South Carolina's and the nation's history. Situated on a particularly beautiful bluff on a fork of the Cooper River, the site was established as a rice plantation in 1681 by a grant to the sons of Sir John Coleton, one of the original "Lords Proprietors" of South Carolina. Then in 1762, the gorgeous property was sold to Henry Laurens, a successful Charleston merchant, planter, statesman. It then became the main residence for Laurens and his wife, Eliza Ball. After several generations of successful rice cultivation, the plantation was sold and passed through various hands until 1936, when it was purchased by renowned publisher Henry R. Luce and his wife, Clare Boothe Luce. It was she, a famous author, congresswoman, and diplomat, who commissioned the beautiful landscape and gardens that we now know, collectively, as the Mepkin Abbey Botanical Garden, a 3,200-acre tract of astonishing natural beauty. The Luces donated Mepkin to the Gethsemani Trappist Abbey in 1949. That year, twenty-nine monks traveled from Kentucky to found Mepkin Abbey.

# Mepkin Abbey

## WHO ARE WE?

*by Father Guerric Heckel, O.C.S.O.*
*Mepkin Abbey Crèche Festival Director*

The community of monks of Mepkin belong to the worldwide "Order of Cistercians of the Strict Observance," popularly known as "Trappists." Following strictly The Rule of St. Benedict, we devote our lives to prayer, spiritual study, work, and hospitality.

For the monks, prayer is unceasing, and infuses all we do. The framework for our monastic daily prayer is the communal celebration of the Eucharist and the Liturgy of the Hours. The "Hours" are those fixed times during the day and night when the monks gather in church to give voice to that inner song of God's praise found in every human heart. The format of the various prayers, which serve as "still points" and root the monks in the "now" of their day, is uniform and simple: an opening verse asking God's assistance in prayer; a hymn appropriate for the day; several psalms from the Old Testament; a reading from Scripture and a concluding prayer. In addition to the Liturgy of the Hours, we devote time to individual and private meditative reading of the Scripture in the morning and evening.

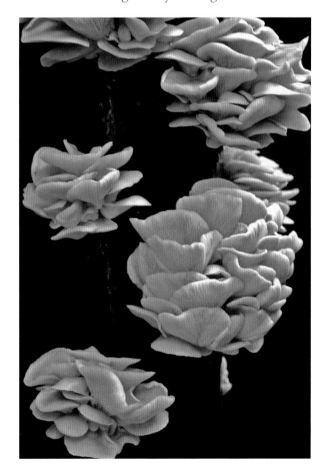

Within this framework of continual prayer and study, Trappists emphasize the spiritual value of hard work. We live by the labor of our hands to provide for ourselves and the poor. The results of our labor can be seen in a variety of products produced on the grounds of the Abbey: Drizzzle, poppy seed dressing, garden compost, and especially White Oyster and Shiitake Mushrooms and micro-greens, which are sold in local stores and featured in select Charleston restaurants. These oyster mushrooms have long been cultivated in Asia for both their medical benefits and excellent taste, and can be purchased, along with books, handcrafted products, and work by regional artisans, in the Mepkin Abbey Store.

We share our spiritual journey and communal lives with all seekers through the hospitality of retreat programs, the Monastic Guest experience, spiritual direction to guests, and by way of guided tours that explain our monastic life. Visitors to Mepkin Abbey can shop at the store, stroll through the Botanical Garden, or see the Clare Boothe Luce Library, funded chiefly by the Henry Luce Foundation and opened in 2001. Providing over 11,000 square feet for a multipurpose facility, the Library houses a monastic collection of some 50,000 volumes (searchable online) on philosophy, theology, monastic studies, and art, as well as a collection of rare books and an archive room. Equipped with the latest in computer technology, the Library also houses a state-of-the-art Conference Center, which was the generous gift of Tom Ashe Lockhart, a descendant of the renowned Henry Laurens. The Library, a true treasure house of wisdom, provides a place where the brothers can study and breathe in the monastic culture and wisdom of many centuries. The monks of Mepkin are also entrusted with the care of the Ugo Tesoriare Collection of original paintings,

the maintenance of the Mepkin Columbarium, while serving as hosts to private and directed spiritual retreats.

It is through these four elements: prayer, study, work, and hospitality that we fulfill our Mission Statement. To respond to God's call; to live in prayer, solitude, and silence and for the Church, according to an ancient form of radical Christian discipleship focused on seeking and finding God in community where we "are of one heart and soul and everything is held in common" (Acts 4: 32-33). We live the Rule of Saint Benedict embodied in the Cistercian tradition, praising God in our prayer, our meditative reading from Scripture, our work, and our hospitality, obeying the call of the Holy Spirit to ceaseless prayer and sharing the sufferings of the present time until the Lord returns (Rm 8: 18-23).

We hope that your time spent with us will be joyous as well as contemplative, whether during your visit to the annual Mepkin Abbey Crèche Festival; a spiritual retreat; a brief stop to absorb the beauty and peace of this sacred space. Here at Mepkin, we extend our arms in praise of our Lord in ceaseless prayer, meditation, or in work.

We extend our arms also in a sincere welcome and blessing to you. Thank you for visiting us, and may the Lord bless and watch over you and yours. We hope that while you are reading this book, you may find your way into the unique ethos of this place and experience some of the aesthetic wonder that the journey through the Mepkin Abbey Crèche Festival has brought to thousands of visitors.

# The Crèche Festival

## A Pilgrim Journey for Today

*by Paul Philibert*

*Paul Philibert, O.P., is a Dominican theologian who has taught at universities both in the U.S. and abroad. He lived for some years at Le Corbusier's monastery, La Tourette, in France, where he came to appreciate modern architecture by living inside it. He is now Promoter of Continuing Studies for the Dominicans in the southern U.S. From 2003 to 2004 he lived at Mepkin Abbey as scholar-in-residence.*

Throughout human history, people across the planet have undertaken journeys seeking special places of bodily healing or sources of spiritual nourishment. Almost all religious traditions include some form of a journey to a holy site — a pilgrimage made by pilgrims.

As the Bible shows us, beginning in the eighth century before Christ, the major religious festivals of the Jews were celebrated at the Temple in Jerusalem. This was the reason for the festival pilgrimages that are reflected even in the life of Jesus many centuries later. For example, it is written that "every year his parents went to Jerusalem for the Festival of the Passover" (Luke 2:14), and "While Jesus was going up to Jerusalem, he took the twelve disciples aside by themselves…" (Matthew 20:18). God was considered to be present in an unparalleled way in the Temple, and to go there at festival time was a great blessing. To this day, something in the human heart has always tried to seek out God's presence and be blessed.

After Christianity became dominant in the ancient Mediterranean world, the places where Jesus walked on earth were defined as sacred places and were sought after by Christians everywhere. For example, in the fourth century, St. Jerome went to Bethlehem and made it his residence during the long years he translated the Bible into Latin.

By the twelfth century there was an acceleration of pilgrimages to visit not only sites directly related to the life of Jesus but also to sites related to saints and to the places of miracles. Such sites within Europe included the shrine of St. James of Compostela (where one of the apostles was buried), the Cathedral of Chartres in France (where there were relics of the Blessed Virgin Mary), and the Cathedral of Canterbury in England (where the martyr St. Thomas Beckett was buried—a pilgrimage made famous by Chaucer's *Canterbury Tales*).

In our secular American culture, it is common to take schoolchildren on field trips to Independence Hall in Philadelphia, to our nation's capital, or to the village of Williamsburg. In all these cases, there is something inspiring about reliving the past in the places where history happened.

### Religious Pilgrimages Today

In recent decades, there has been a revival of these religious pilgrimages. Every year both individuals and groups undertake the pilgrimage on foot, on bicycles, and even on horseback to Compostela in northwest Spain. They undertake this journey of hundreds of miles from locations throughout Europe. The pilgrims traverse a landscape on pathways used for centuries. They visit shrines, monasteries, and cathedrals that have been official way stations for ages. All the while the pilgrims experience the beauty of nature, from the soaring peaks of the Pyrenees to the sea-washed stone of Compostela.

Today devout Roman Catholics continue to make pilgrimages to Lourdes, to Fatima, to Medjugorje and to the Mexican shrine of Our Lady of Guadalupe. Possibly the expectations and the travels themselves are as rewarding and life-changing as the brief days or hours spent at the particular shrine. As was the case for Chaucer's pilgrims on the road to medieval Canterbury, contemporary pilgrims make new friends, learn interesting stories, see new sites and return home refreshed, blessed, and open to new ideas.

## A MEPKIN PILGRIMAGE

In 2002, Mepkin Abbey launched its own event that has grown into an annual celebration of Advent and Christmas — the Crèche Festival. The monks assembled a varied collection of nativity sets representing different races, cultures, and artistic traditions. The majority of the collection began with donations by individuals, including a collection of over 400 crèches given to Mepkin by Earl Kage of Rochester, New York. Churches and friends continue to add to the Mepkin collection. Recently Mepkin commissioned contemporary artists to create modern interpretations of the Christmas event especially for the collection.

The Crèche Festival explores the questions raised by the exhibition itself: How has the sacred moment of miraculous birth been portrayed in sculpture through the ages? How have various cultures and nations defined the event? How can a collection of sculptural figures communicate fundamental religious experiences with new vitality to the modern viewer who is so familiar with the stereotypical scene of the Christmas nativity? What unique physical characteristics have been given to the figures of the shepherd, the magi, the angels and the Holy Family? How does the presentation of the event of the birth reflect the point of view of the artist who created the sculptures?

The crèche exhibit answers such questions directly and concretely by using a visual vocabulary derived from Mepkin's international collection. Some crèches are dramatic and theatrical, like the large Neapolitan crèche that rivals scenery for a Baroque opera. Others are intimate and inspirational, like the Latin American figures of the Holy Family that suggest contemporary campesinos (poor farm workers). Still other crèches have classical nobility, like a crèche donated by a monastery

in France in which the characters seem to emerge from the sculptured frieze of a Romanesque church in the region known as the French midi.

Each display attempts to say something revelatory — not only about the mystery of God's Incarnation in Jesus Christ but also about whatever it is within us that seeks and yearns for the discovery of God present in our world. Theological ideas that are firm but fairly abstract become concrete in seeing that Christ's Incarnation is meant to touch every culture and inform the whole of our universal humanity. In this way, we see a baby Jesus who was not only Caucasian but Asian and Indian and African and Latin American as well. We see some Mothers of God who look European and svelte, but others who look ethnic and poor and awed and powerful and humble.

In addition, the Mepkin Crèche Festival is presented in a setting that suggests a natural labyrinth with curving avenues of large evergreen trees. The crèches are displayed in a manner that allows the visitors an opportunity to make discoveries as they follow the pilgrimage route through the "woods." The conference room of the Mepkin Library is transformed into an environment that attempts to lead the viewer to explore emotions of mystery, wonder, joy, surprise, and even humor.

In some way, each visitor/pilgrim who comes to Mepkin ends up seeing the Nativity with new eyes. For those with Christian faith, each one is moved to a deeper understanding of the mystery of God's love for humanity.

## What Lies Beneath the Pilgrim's Experience?

Curiosity and adventure also have their part to play in the success of the Mepkin crèche exhibition. For example, the contemporary pilgrims might wonder what such an art installation could possibly create, especially for them. They are inquisitive about the way in which a familiar idea can be translated into novel shapes and forms. This is an exhibition, after all, and as such, it never disappoints. Many of those who come have come before, eager to take the opportunity to prepare themselves for Christmas with this very down-to-earth meditation on the birth of Christ.

But adventure plays a part as well. For many visitors, this is their first visit to a monastery. Finding a beautiful place, an orderly arrangement of monastic buildings in a profoundly tranquil setting, and seeing the locale for a life of penance and silence and prayer is an eye-opener. The exhibition is a form of hospitality extended to visitors by the monks, sharing their place and their vision of a world penetrated by grace.

But can we really call this a pilgrimage, after all? A pilgrimage presupposes a journey to an encounter with the holy and a transformation of the pilgrim.

Well, you decide. Are there feelings and hopes inside you that you don't know how to name? Are there concerns that hunger for the reassurance that the world carries within it a saving blessing to redeem us? Are you perhaps a Christian whose sense of religious life has become almost tiresomely routine? Are you enticed by the possibility that beauty — simple sculptural beauty — can quicken your sensibilities and renew your faith?

Are you attracted by the idea of preparing for Christmas by doing something special that will tune your soul into the graced promise of the season of Advent? Are you carrying a burden of grief or sadness that weighs upon your heart? Are you adventuresome? Do you want to see if, just possibly, a festival of faith might make the strings of your heart vibrate again? Are you a simple believer who wants to pay homage to the Lord and Master who came at Christmas to sanctify our world? If the answer to any of these questions is yes, then, yes, you are a pilgrim.

Bring to the Crèche Festival all the questions and all the hopes that you carry in your life. Like everyone else who comes here, you too are still an unfinished person in an incomplete world. You don't need to fully know exactly what you believe. You don't need to be a faithful Sunday churchgoer. You don't need to commit yourself to any creeds or statements about Jesus or the church to be welcome here. Come as you are and observe.

But when you come, do open your eyes and open your heart. Maybe you will just be fascinated. Maybe you will be amazed at the artistry. Maybe you will soon forget what you see. Maybe you will be pleasantly charmed and haunted by some image or feeling that is awakened in your visit. In any case, what happens in your heart may not easily translate directly into words. There is a density of feeling and knowing in any artistic experience. You will carry away with you a seed of new life, that is, a seed for your new life — your life for tomorrow. It will grow and sprout and possibly blossom all in due time. It may surprise you. Pilgrim memories are rich . . . and deep.

When you return home, take along with you the joy and the beauty, the promise and the hope of what the crèche exhibition contains. You will take with you as well the prayers, good wishes, and the blessings of the monks of Mepkin Abbey.

Peace.

## Birth and Renewal

The divine child calls to us, pilgrims journeying to this sacred place. The pilgrimage is porous, inviting, and inclusive. Far-flung ancient cultures, various religions, and disparate ethnicities share the common story of people on quests for salvation. What members of the world community will join in to share this joyous celebration of a birth?

In my sculptural interpretation, the Christ child is offered on a humble bed. Diverse believers of all orientations surround Him, forming the inner circle of a pattern radiating outward to infinity. In Buddhist culture, the lotus represents the origin of life, the womb of the universe. The alternating and concentric circles of human forms and hands that form the lotus blossom suggest reflection, song, and solemn dance. Hopeful hands raise the precious story to the light of God; these grateful pilgrims invite us to participate.

ANNA KOLOSEIKE
ASHEVILLE, NORTH CAROLINA

# The History of the Mepkin Abbey Crèche Festival

### by Father Guerric Heckel, O.C.S.O.
#### Mepkin Abbey Crèche Festival Director

*As a monk, Father Guerric Heckel is the store manager and director of the Mepkin Abbey Crèche Festival. He came to the Abbey in 1994 after being a parish priest for 28 years and serving as a hospital chaplain for 11 of those years. He has had a love for crèches since childhood.*

When I came to the monastery in 1994, I never expected that I would be in retail sales or have the opportunity to pursue one of my loves, the Christmas Crèche. But when I became manager of our Mepkin Abbey Store in 2002, I had the opportunity to do both.

Since I had always believed that people should be able to purchase a nice crèche in a monastery store, I proceeded to order $5,000 worth of crèches at the first trade show I attended. As a result, my store board advised me to do an exhibit of crèches to encourage people to come to the store and purchase their own. The monastery had 10 lovely sets for display at our first exhibition, and Al Walker, a friend and antiques dealer from Boston, loaned and donated 10 additional sets for display in the conference room of our library. Additionally, Rev. Msgr. Philip J. Franceschini from Our Lady of Pity Parish in Staten Island, New York, loaned us his beautiful Neapolitan set to round out the display. With 30 sets in all, we began to plan for our first festival in the fall of 2002.

Fortunately for me, on the Store's Board we had a landscape designer, Judith Kramer, and Arthur McDonald, the retired Chair of the Fine Arts Department at the College of Charleston. Judith offered to do a forest-like design with real cedar, loblolly pine, and magnolia trees, and Arthur offered to stage the Nativity sets.

With everything in place, we hastily sent out a flyer to all the folks on our mailing list, inviting them to visit our "Nativity Sets from Around the World." To our delight, some 1,500 people attended that first exhibit, and we knew then that we had struck upon an idea with a broad appeal to the general public. So we planned to do a second Crèche festival in 2003.

In yet another fortunate turn of events, Peggy Savlo, a board member, acquainted us with her friend, Earl Kage, a crèche collector from Rochester, New York. We asked Earl if we might borrow 50 of his crèches to exhibit in the Second Annual Mepkin Abbey "Crèche Festival." We had chosen this name in order to include lectures and other related events as part of the exhibit itself.

When Earl Kage arrived and saw how stunning the exhibit was, and how beautifully his crèches were displayed, he proceeded to donate his whole collection of over 400 crèches to the Abbey! Since we would be showing 40 to 50 crèches at each Festival, we knew it would take a few years to show his collection in its entirety. And because attendance had doubled the second year, we were convinced of the ongoing appeal of the Festival as an annual event. 2003 was also the year we produced the video Nativity: "The Art and Spirit of the Crèche," which aired on PBS stations throughout the country and featured Mepkin Abbey's crèches. (The DVD is available in our store or online at www.mepkinabbey.org.)

After completing their tour, many of the visitors stood in line at the store, tears in their eyes, as they recalled the crèches they so loved and cherished in their childhood. By bringing back these beautiful childhood memories, we knew that Mepkin's Crèche Festival had touched a deep and tender place in the hearts of people. In addition, having the Festival on weekends before and after Thanksgiving proved to be a reflective way to begin the celebration of Christmas. Not surprisingly, attending the annual Crèche Festival at Mepkin Abbey has become a popular and cherished tradition.

Regardless of personal background or culture, visitors will see their own faces in these crèches, and will experience the universal spiritual gift and power of Christ's birth. It is thrilling to witness how artists around the world have incorporated the dress, animals, and features of their own country and heritage, and their creativity and use of unusual materials are always surprising.

Even though Mepkin does not charge admission to the Festival, people are generous in making donations and submissions to cover the cost. With these funds we are able to commission artists to create additional crèches for our Festival, and it has been very inspiring to see how contemporary artists depict such an ancient religious event. Also, our insistence on using all natural materials for our display has, I think, touched people's desire for the "real" in contrast to the "plastic" world in which we live. For example, the owner of a local nursery, along with her family and staff, spent weeks gathering natural materials to make a 10-foot wreath to hang from Mepkin's library tower. And as we become better known for our Festival, folks are giving or loaning special crèches to Mepkin's collection, providing yet another chance to appreciate the creativity found in this form of Folk Art.

Another exciting outcome of our Festival is that several churches have created their own Festival, and invite parishioners to bring a favorite Nativity set to the church hall for display. Recently, we instituted the practice of asking visitors: "Which crèche is your favorite?" This has proved to be an effective way to encourage closer attention to details, and gives evidence of what elements visitors most respond to.

In 17 days of the 2011 Festival, some 7,000 people attended! So in order to make the Festival more reflective, we decided to limit the number of visitors to 70 each half-hour. Up to and including the Thanksgiving weekend, the reservations are limited to groups of ten or less, and we reserve the week after Thanksgiving for larger group tours. In this way we try to accommodate larger groups and yet keep the "reflective nature" of the exhibit intact.

I would be remiss by not mentioning one of the wonderful by-products of the Crèche Festival: the dedicated groups of some 70 volunteers who come each year. It is their generosity, hard work, and genuine hospitality that have helped make the Crèche Festival a real gift to the community, providing its thousands of visitors with the wonderful opportunity to grow in a deeper and warmer understanding of THE NATIVITY.

When the song of the angels is stilled,
When the star in the sky is gone,
When the kings and princes are home,
When the shepherds are back with their flock,
The work of Christmas begins:
To find the lost,
To heal the broken,
To feed the hungry,
To release the prisoner,
To rebuild the nations,
To bring peace among people,
To make music in the heart.

HOWARD THURMAN

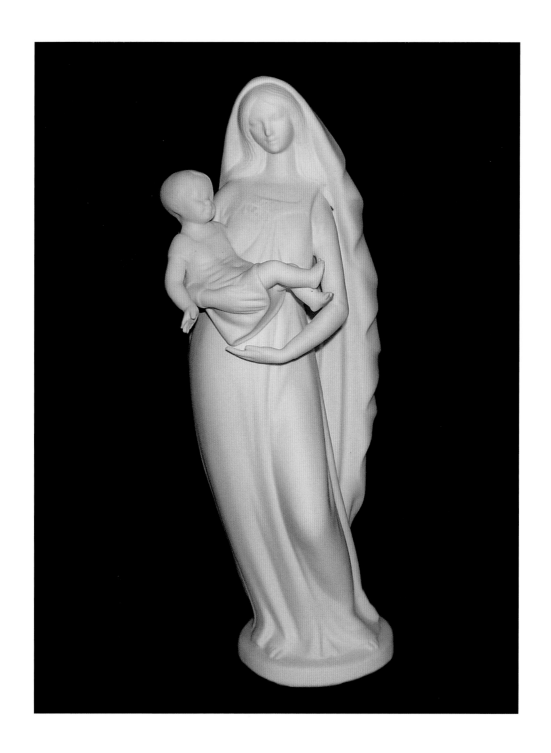

## Nativity

I marvel at the universality of art and the power it has to connect those of us who do not speak the same creative language. As a result, my goal as an artist is to pull an emotional response from the viewer, and to speak to them through clay, through glass, or through a piece of discarded metal that finds its way into my work. In this way I can bring them the world that I observe and experience in the hope that they will find a moment of repose, a sense of beauty, or an alternative perspective.

I was once told by my mentor that to know something one must draw it. I find that same experience true through the medium of clay. As I create the folds of a garment or the gesture of a figure, I come to know the story more deeply. I try to understand, through the mind's eye, what Mary and Joseph must have felt that night, or what the mood might have been. It is my hope to invoke a sense of haste and anticipation through this Nativity – a moment in time when Mary and Joseph are just starting their journey, leaving the relative safety of their shelter, Jesus wrapped securely in His mother's arms, with a few companions to help them along the way.

ANGEL ALLEN
COLUMBIA, SOUTH CAROLINA

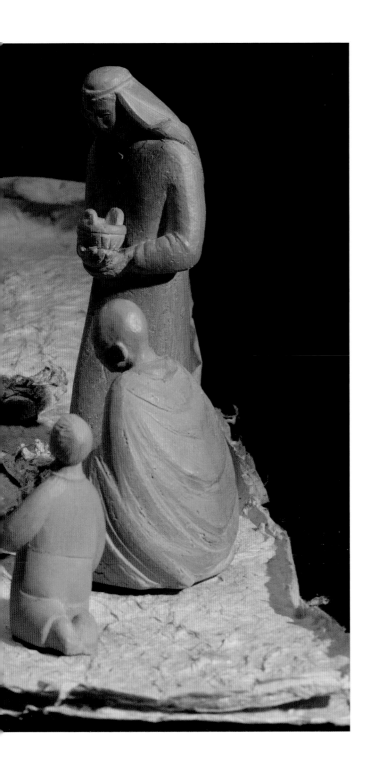

$M$ay every age return to a blessed infancy
and be conformed to You
not in weakness of body
but in humility of intellect
and holiness of purpose.

BLESSED GUERRIC OF IGNY
SERMON I, CHRISTMAS

48

He is born in Bethlehem in order that He may be born in us. He gives Himself to us as a child in order to share with us not only His infant smiles and caresses, but above all His very birth and infancy. He is born Son of Man in order that we may be born sons of God, our souls being Bethlehems in which He is born 'for us, . . .

BLESSED GUERRIC OF IGNY
CHRISTMAS SERMONS

# The Story of the Nativity

## AS TOLD AROUND THE WORLD

*by Earl Kage*

*Earl Kage was once called "a one-man cultural resource" in a newspaper profile. When he retired from Eastman Kodak, where he was a manager of the Kodak Research Studio, Kage devoted his energies to a second career as a photographer and a number of community interests. He collected crèches for nearly 50 years.*

Whether it's placed under the Christmas tree, on a table, or on the fireplace mantel, the crib or manger scene has been a part of family Christmas decorations for generations. While the Christmas tree with its ornamentation is of German origin, the Nativity scene originated in the Catholic countries of southern Europe. Both of these decorative devices have been known since the 16th century, but the traditions from which they were derived are much older.

A decorative tree at Christmastime was first reported about 1520 in Alsatia (later known as Alsace-Lorraine). The tree, which was adorned with fruit, cakes, glass balls, and candles, represented the fusion of two different religious customs of the Middle Ages: the paradise tree and the Christmas light. The paradise tree, brought into the house on December 24 and hung with red apples, was an allusion to the tree in the Garden of Eden and to Adam and Eve, whose feast day was celebrated the day before Christmas. The Christmas light was a large candle or group of candles lit on Holy Night to symbolize the birth of Christ and the light that shone over Bethlehem at the Nativity. From Alsatia, the custom of decorating a tree with both of these elements then spread rapidly throughout Germany, and by the beginning of the 18th century, the custom was brought to America by the first German immigrants. During the 19th century it was introduced into France and later became popular in Victorian England.

The manger scene by its many names — French crèche, Italian presepio, German krippe, Spanish belen, or Southwest American nacimiento — has an even more ancient and complex heritage: it is a visualization of the birth of Christ going back to

the first renderings of the Nativity found on sarcophagi of the 4th century. Two centuries later, a small chapel in the Basilica of Santo Maria Maggiore in Rome was devoted to crib relics for pilgrim worship. And hundreds of years after that, in 1223, Saint Francis created a live tableau in the forest at Greccio, a village near Assisi. After placing a child in a straw-filled feeding trough and leading an ass and an ox into the scene, he then retold the Gospel story to an audience thrilled with the recreation. The earliest freestanding representations, however, probably occurred in 1291, when carved figures of Jesus, Mary, and Joseph were added to the display.

The construction and arrangement of the crèche was originally a devotional practice of the Jesuits, who in 1560-62 built the first examples in Coimbra, Portugal, and in Prague. In these examples, artisans carved and modeled figures of great realism from stone, wood, and terra-cotta. Originally the scene consisted of only three figures—Jesus, Mary, and Joseph. Later the three kings were included, and still later, animals, an angel, and shepherds. It also became a tradition in nativity scenes that the representation of the baby Jesus be added to the scene on Christmas Eve, with the three kings being added on the Feast of the Epiphany, or Twelfth Night. In the early 1560s, the first known crèche made specifically for a home was commissioned by the Duchess of Amalfi for her personal Christmas celebration. Soon the building of these crèches became a practice throughout the Italian peninsula, especially in Genoa, Sicily, and Naples, where by 1670 the leading families kept open house for the viewing of their elaborate presepios.

The depiction reached even greater artistic heights in 1750, however, when artists would be invited directly into the homes of prosperous homeowners to create unique crèches. In time, this concept spread throughout Europe as the Italian artisans sent their works overland by way of peddlers and travelers. Examples of some of these earliest crèches are in the collections of the Bayerisches National Museum in Munich and the Museo di San Martino

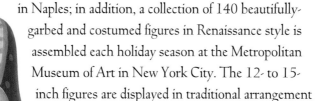

in Naples; in addition, a collection of 140 beautifully-garbed and costumed figures in Renaissance style is assembled each holiday season at the Metropolitan Museum of Art in New York City. The 12- to 15-inch figures are displayed in traditional arrangement to enhance a 30-foot Christmas tree.

Interpretations of the Nativity vary greatly, and it is this diversity that has made each recreation of the basic Christmas story greatly intriguing to me, and has always sustained my interest in the collection. For example, one of my favorite manger scenes is the French santons crèche. Created by craftsmen in the Provence region of southern France, the brightly painted earthenware figures are known as santons, or little saints. First appearing in the early 19th century, the figures are still made today and depict customs that still endure. The central figures are the traditional Jesus, Mary, and Joseph along with the three kings, an angel, and animals. But the surrounding pieces are representations of 19th-century villagers — including woodsmen, tailors, basket-makers, knife-grinders, and even a bear tamer.

In many of the manger scenes, Jesus is shown with arms outstretched in the manner of early paintings. In others, the baby is tightly wrapped with only his face showing. Also included in some of the scenes is a rooster, or a lily in the hand of Joseph — both symbols of birth or new life.

Since the Renaissance, artists have depicted the manger scene as if it were native to their times, peoples, and countries. Many of the scenes in this collection reflect this tradition. The larger Colombian terra-cotta figures appear as local townspeople; the manger from Cochiti Pueblo, New Mexico, features Native American dress; and the 1950 Spanish nacimiento, by Manuel Vigil of Tesuque Pueblo, dresses Joseph in a Spanish sombrero and boots with a cross around his neck.

But even in its simplest form — the Holy Family alone — the seasonal display of the Nativity is a means of engaging the emotions of the faithful and heightening the intensity of the spiritual experience. For Christians, it is a special time — and a special way to reflect on this great moment of peace and joy.

*Joy is the most infallible sign
of the presence of God.*

TEILHARD DE CHARDIN

59

## Hammered Coppered Nativity

The crèche that I have been creating for Mepkin Abbey over the past few years is made from formed and brazed sheet copper. I am using .032" thickness (24 oz.) to give more weight to the figures and for greater stretch ability. Copper is very malleable and can be worked cold. With repeated annealing, it can be hammered and tooled into quite intricate forms. The figures are built up piece by piece, forming and fitting, and brazing together with phosphor-copper rods and oxi-acetylene torch. I like copper as a medium for its versatility and warmth of color.

I have tried to create an experience of joy and wonder and awe at the birth of God as man, the dawn of our salvation, in the gestures of the various figures of the crèche. The traditional animals add variety and interest and give the rest of God's creation a place in the redemption.

MARY ELDREDGE
SPRINGFIELD, VERMONT

61

It comes every year and will go on forever. And along
with Christmas belong the keepsakes and the customs.
Those humble, everyday things a mother clings to,
and ponders, like Mary in the secret spaces of her heart.

MARJORIE HOLMES

*What can I give Him,*
*Poor as I am?*
*If I were a shepherd*
*I would bring a lamb.*
*If I were a Wise Man*
*I would do my part.*
*Yet what can I give Him?*
*I give Him my heart.*

CHRISTINA ROSSETTI

M*ankind is a great,*
*an immense family . . .*
*This is proved by what we feel*
*in our hearts at Christmas.*

POPE JOHN XXIII

69

# Nativity Folk Art

## A PILGRIM JOURNEY FOR TODAY

*by Frances Anderson*

*Dr. Frances E. Anderson, ATR-BC, HLM (Board Certified Art Therapist), is Distinguished Professor of Art Emerita, Illinois State University, and Affiliate Faculty, College of Charleston. She is a clay artist, photographer, and recipient of five Fulbright Awards (Argentina 2002, Taiwan 2004, Thailand 2008, and Pakistan (twice) 2010) for research and teaching. She has been collecting folk art crèches globally since 1980.*

The words *nativity* and *crèche* (the French word for crib) are often used interchangeably. Folk art crèches present Mary, Joseph, and Christ in a stable or some other shelter. Often some (or all) of the other traditional figures, including the three kings, shepherds, animals, and angels, are included as well. There is no specific rubric or pattern, and the kind and number of figures depend on the artist and on his or her culture. However, in all of these nativities the centerpiece is the Holy Family. Folk art nativities also combine the characteristics of a specific culture while expressing a worldwide theme, the birth of Christ. This combination of a universal theme, executed with traditional, locally available materials, provides us with a wonderful means of cultural comparison; the variety of depictions of Christ's birth is amazing.

Nativity folk artists often infuse their creations with an energy and spirituality that becomes a magnet, drawing the viewer to them in a unique way. One's heart "jumps" when observing how the birth of Christ is reflected through different cultural eyes.

For example, a nativity from the Caribbean has figures with dreadlocks, whereas a scene from China shows figures with Asian eyes. An African crèche presents figures in traditional Masai tribal dress, while a crèche from Peru shows Mary and the Christ Child lying in a traditional Peruvian bed, with Joseph and the shepherds standing beside it. A crèche from Madagascar includes animals found only in that area; a Guatemalan crèche dresses its figures in hand woven cloth found only in that country. An Indian crèche has culturally traditional designs on the clothing of the figures. A Pakistani crèche's figures are made in the form of individual wood blocks with raised copper details, which could be used to make block prints of each figure. (This type of block printing is traditional in both the Pakistani and the Indian cultures.) A hammock is the manger for Christ in a crèche from Indonesia.

Unfortunately, it is becoming increasingly difficult to find folk art nativities that are not influenced by external commercial interests. Let us hope that these folk art creations represented in the Mepkin Abbey Crèche Festival continue to be made, and that their artists resist outside influences and instead reflect on their own unique cultures and history.

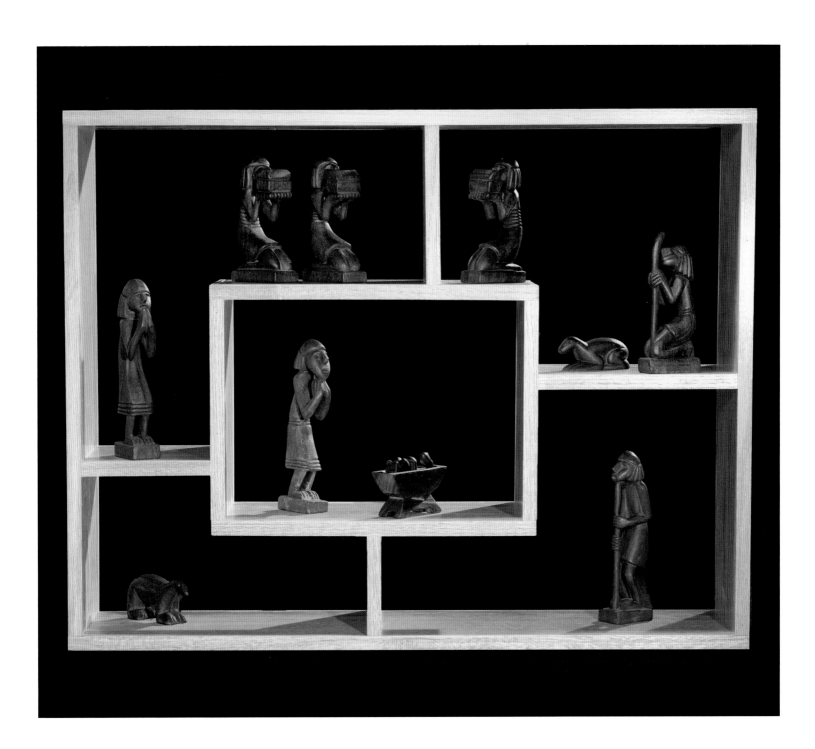

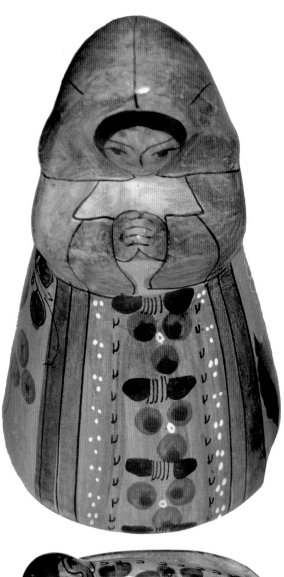

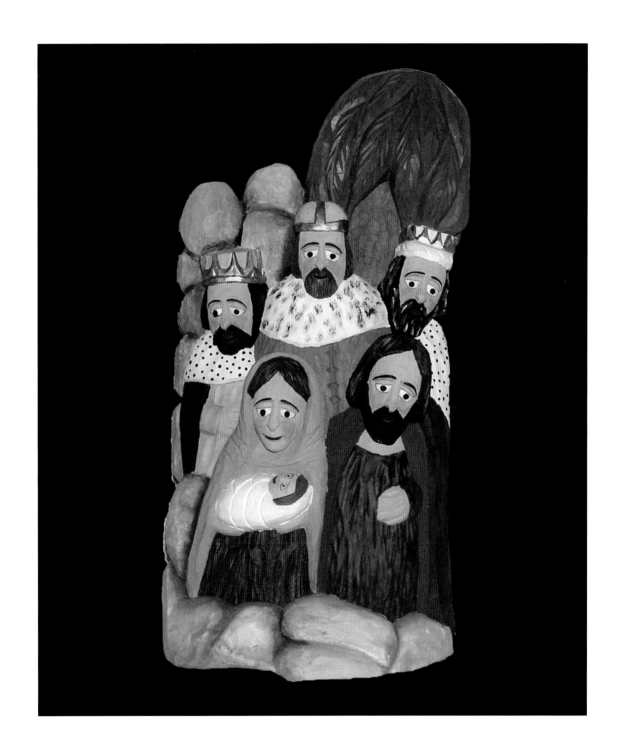

# Designing a Journey of Anticipation

*by Judith Kramer*

*Judith Kramer is an Environmental Designer with a particular interest
in creating sacred space -- that place where art and spirit intersect.*

It was summer of 2002 when, during an otherwise normal business meeting, an excited exchange regarding the possibility of a crèche festival at Mepkin Abbey occurred. Here was a way the monks of Mepkin could comfortably extend their ethic of hospitality, inviting more of the public in to experience this beautiful and iconic Low-Country jewel—a jewel steeped in both history and a sense of place.

As an Environmental Designer, I was asked to design a "container" within the confines of the new Mepkin Abbey Library Conference Room, through which a display of individual crèche scenes could be viewed, one at a time. Instinctively, I envisioned a wall of green and a circuitous path determining the placement of tables and exhibits, creating an unfolding progression of crèche scenes. This path would be similar to a labyrinth in which we view only that which is directly in front of us, while the meandering path would obscure what lies ahead. In this way, a sense of mystery and anticipation would build as we continued along the path.

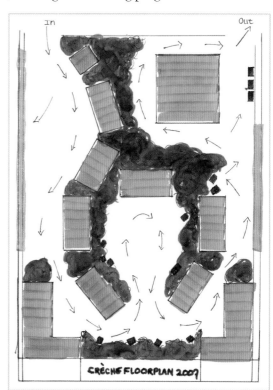

Toward this end a group of dedicated volunteers cut, sprayed against early wilt, and set up dozens of native Eastern Red Cedar and Loblolly pine trees. Potted dwarf magnolias were donated and interspersed as textural accents and as screens for the ends of tables. All this greenery, gathered together in the Conference Room, transformed the room with its honey-colored vaulted ceiling and white walls into a veritable forest, which we then further enhanced with muted light, music, and the scent of Christmas. All tree pots and stands were camouflaged by puddling black cloth over them. The path among these walls then became the backdrop for the tables and pedestals used as display surfaces.

Natural white sailcloth was used to cover all tables to the floor, creating a neutral canvas for Arthur McDonald's original placement of the various figurines and their props. When Arthur's work was complete, hundreds of candles were added to the tables and pedestals. Rolled together, all these elements provided a hushed and reverent space in which the story of Christmas was retold in scores of different ways. The participants that first year were deeply moved, and we knew we had created something quite special.

This original design concept has been largely repeated every year for nine years. The overall shape, with its twists and turns and multileveled display surfaces, has shifted a bit each year to accommodate the particular group of crèches being displayed. This has kept the crèche experience fresh for those of us composing it as well as for the visitors who return year after year, anxious to re-experience their delight within the folds of this exquisite space.

Originally, the journey to the Mepkin Abbey Crèche Exhibit began at the Abbey Store and proceeded directly through St. Clare's garden and on to the library via the stairs under the bridge. Today the crèche experience starts at the store and slowly unfurls along a winding garden path, up the drive to the abbey, through the breezeway and on to the library. Here and there along the way outdoor nativity sets are tucked in among the permanent plantings and trees, further enhancing a delicious anticipation and sense of mystery for what lies ahead inside.

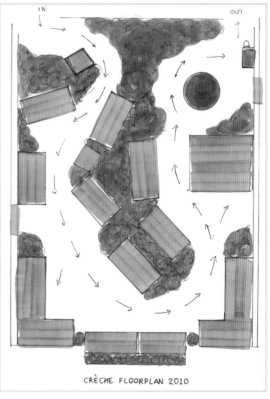

CRÈCHE FLOORPLAN 2010

The design and construction process now begins in February, when the year's display of individual crèches is chosen. The size and number chosen will then dictate how I sketch out the path and tentatively place tables and other surfaces on a design. The number of trees needed to outline the path is already determined, though it has tended to increase every year! From this point, any new display surfaces such as pedestals or shelving units needed for the current year's display are contracted to be built, and any additional material for tables and pots ordered. When all these are finally pulled together, we are ready to transform the library in the beginning of November.

A full week is needed to clear the library of chairs and extra tables, gather the trees, install them among the tables, cover the tables, drape the pots and stands, install all the crèche figurines, the candles, and the consecutive numbers for the program, and clean up and be ready for the preview walk by the monks on Saturday night before the Benefactors Concert. It is a wonderful, collaborative effort of scores of people leading up to this candlelit walk through a familiar yet totally transformed space. Judging from the many comments overheard or received directly, it is an experience-turned-holiday ritual by many, of all faiths, from far and wide.

I have enjoyed, and am grateful for, the continued design challenge and the sense of satisfaction we all feel when we have completed yet another fabulous Mepkin Abbey Annual Crèche Festival. The personal reward for me is the sense that I have contributed spiritually and materially, in some small way, to the ongoing existence of an ancient and extraordinary way of life, a way of life made a bit more visible to us all by the increased accessibility of the public to this amazingly beautiful place.

$T$he great mystery of the Incarnation, which meant that God became man so that men might become God, was a joy that made us want to kiss the earth in worship because his feet once trod the same earth.

DOROTHY DAY
THE LONG LONELINESS

The whole purpose of the celebration of
Christmas is not the commemoration
of Christ's birth but the renewal of this
grace of rebirth and spiritual infancy in
the hearts of the faithful. This consists
first of all in a new realization that our
Christ-life is a gift of the infinite mercy
of God.   It means also a renewal of
gratitude for His generosity.   It means
new joy in His love.   These are the
particular means by which the grace
of Christmas energizes our spirit and
enables us to receive a fresh increase
of charity and supernatural life.

THOMAS MERTON

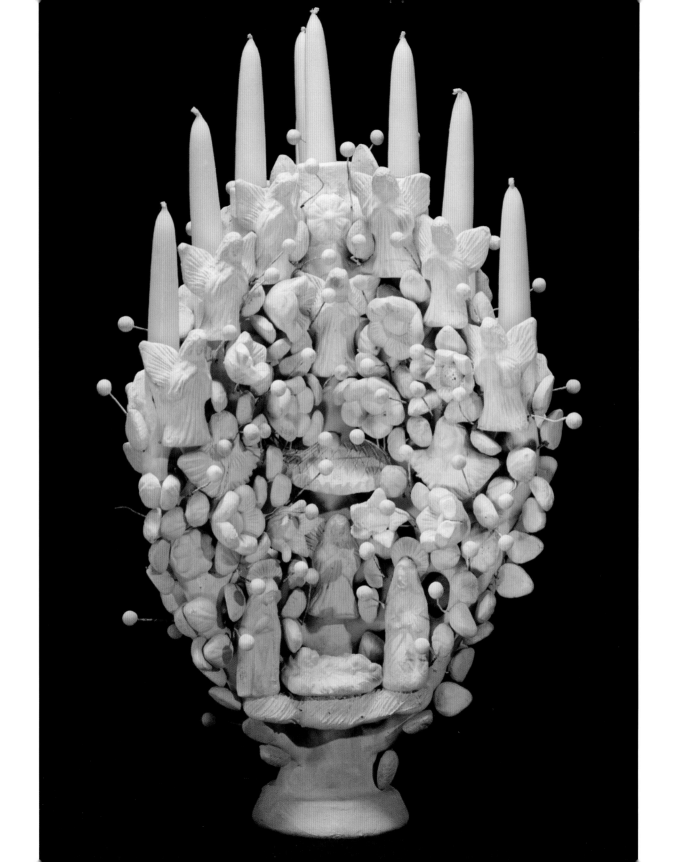

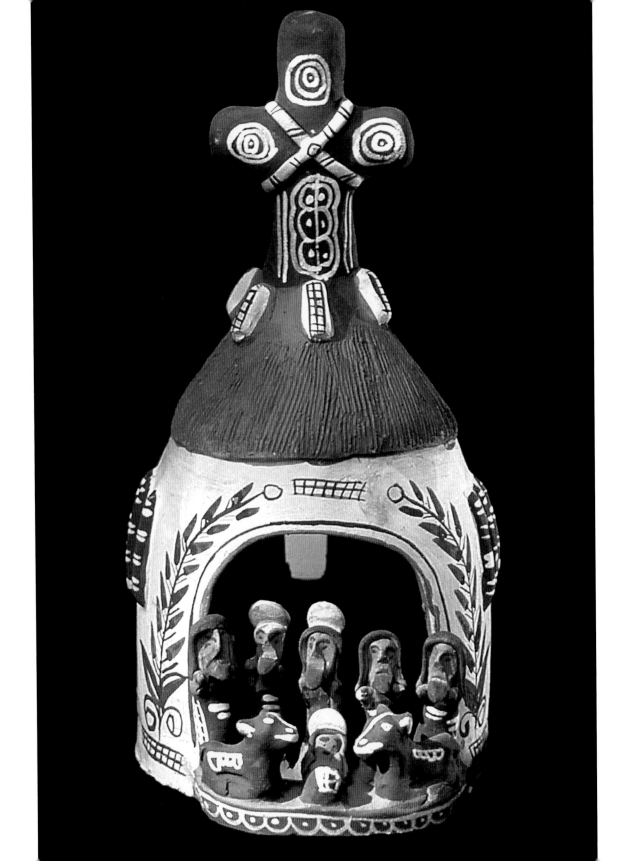

## The Nativity in Clay

I have been working with clay for more than thirty years, but I really never considered myself a sculptor. I suppose ultimately pottery is a form of sculpting, even if it is bowls, cups, or statuary such as my "watchers," open-faced figures resembling monks. But trying to make life-like figures has been a whole new venture for me.

When Mepkin Abbey commissioned me to create statues of Mary and Joseph for the annual crèche festival I quickly agreed without thinking! It was only later that it dawned on me what I had agreed to do, and the journey has been rich with exploration and learning. I had never actually made faces before, and my first efforts were less than pleasing. But through reading, watching videos, and asking questions, I learned to make a head separate from a body, and then attach it. Joseph was my first real success, and as he emerged, I found myself laughing—he was becoming real indeed. (I think he even laughed back!)

From the beginning, I saw Joseph as holding Jesus, rather than the traditional seated Mary holding the baby while Joseph stood in the background. It seemed to me that Joseph also would be filled with wonder at this miraculous event, and like any father, he would delight in holding this miraculous child. After all, an angel had told him this birth was to be more than special. I have tried to convey this, with Mary looking on, smiling, yet filled with questions as to what all of this will mean.

SYBIL WEST
WRIGHTSVILLE BEACH, NORTH CAROLINA

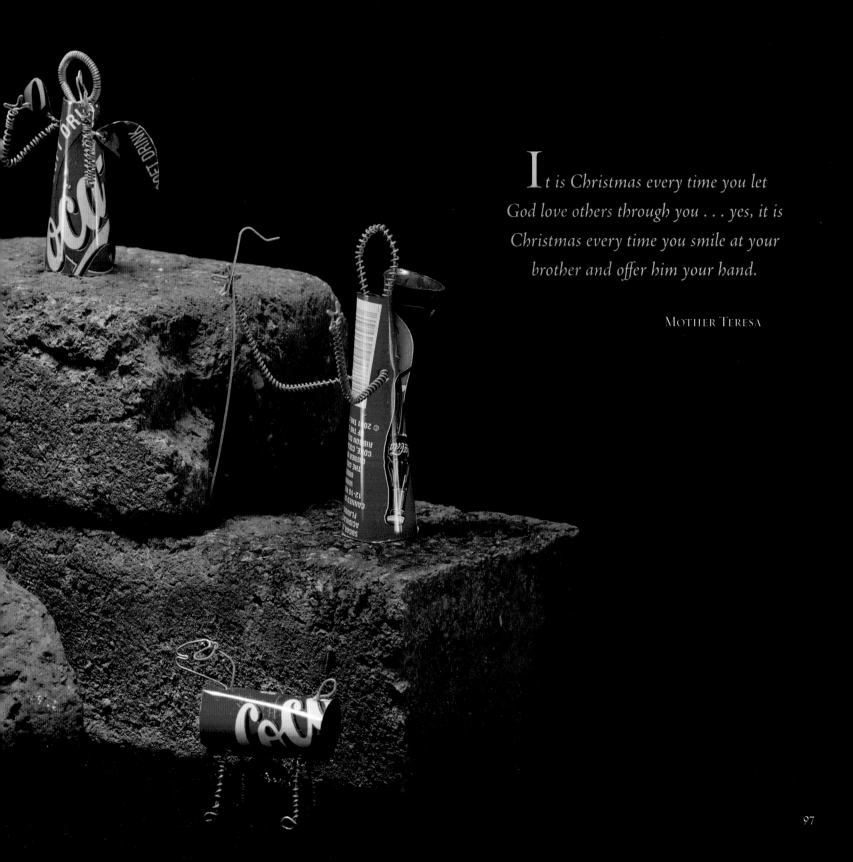

$I$t is Christmas every time you let
God love others through you . . . yes, it is
Christmas every time you smile at your
brother and offer him your hand.

MOTHER TERESA

# Nativity as Narrative

by Arthur W. McDonald
Distinguished Professor Emeritus of Theatre
College of Charleston

*After a career in the performing arts, Arthur turned to the visual arts. For over a decade he has studied and practiced the art of Asian papermaking. He has exhibited his artwork throughout the southeastern United States; most important, he had two works in an exhibition in Kentucky entitled: "The Healing Power of Art." In January 2011 his work was exhibited in a group show in two locations in Korea, and on two occasions he was an artist-in-residence in a papermaking studio in northern Thailand. He has also visited and studied papermaking in Bhutan, Burma, Cambodia, Laos, and the Yunnan province of China.*

Until the mid-14th century, the city of York, England, celebrated the annual Festival of Corpus Christi and included, as part of the pageantry, the presentation and viewing of plays. This theatrical aspect of the festival took place on a series of pageant wagons that were paraded in sequence through the city much like floats in a modern parade. At select locations, the pageant wagons would stop, and the actors would present a short play designed to recount a scene from biblical history. By the end of the day, viewers would have watched more than 50 different plays—all of which were performed with no scenery and minimal props.

As a theater historian arranging the Nativity scenes at Mepkin's annual Crèche Festival, I have often reflected on the York Corpus Christi cycle and its presentation of religious drama. The pageant wagons, by necessity, focused the viewer's attention on the actors in the play, and I try to achieve this same effect through my design of the individual Nativity scenes on their pedestals and tabletops. There are numerous details that I consider when selecting where each crèche should be placed within the overall exhibit. I begin by deciding where each of the crèches should be placed in relation to one another, and whether they will share a table or be isolated on a pedestal. I may group several crèches that are similar in size, texture, and color, such as three crèches from the American Southwest. I may, on the other hand, cluster very different looking crèches that are constructed of similar materials, such as an unadorned wooden crèche from Nigeria and a vibrant wooden crèche from Russia. I may display in tandem two crèches of very dissimilar materials, such as a solid marble crèche from Italy and a Malian Nativity constructed from discarded cans. Or, I may juxtapose a minimalist Nativity scene such as "Epiphany" by Carl Zollo that consists of heads on two oval bronze pieces with an extremely detailed crèche such as the Laotian one with its elephants, monkeys, and houses on stilts. Through these placements, I hope to intensify the viewer's focus on the various national and cultural interpretations of the scene while simultaneously inviting the viewer to contemplate the universality that permeates all depictions of the Nativity.

Once I have determined the placement of the crèches, I decide on a material such as rock, fabric, or paper to use to define the boundaries of the Nativity scenes and to direct the viewer's focus to the figures that comprise a specific scene. Even though there

is spontaneity to the arrangement of the figures, I never place one of them without giving thought to how it is turned and where it is placed in relationship to the other figures. I may position the figures in their traditional placements, or I may choose a staging that does not support the traditional relationship. I may include rocks, gnarls of wood, or other natural elements, or I may leave the scene devoid of any props. These choices are deliberate, and through them, I encourage the viewer to ask questions about the iconic figures, the placement of the figures in relation to one another, and the myriad of other subtle variations in the scenes. In most of the Nativity scenes, I maintain the intrinsic focus on the Christ child; however, there are times when the nature of a crèche requires that I broaden the focus. For instance, a few of the crèches include more than 200 figures ranging from wise men to wandering minstrels. As I arrange these figures, I sometimes choose to obscure the location of the stable so that the viewer, like the shepherds and wise men, must actively seek out the location of the Christ child within the context of the larger world.

At all stages of the display design process, I am continually aware of the need to engage the viewer in the individual scenes as well as in the collective display. In this sense, the crèches are like the medieval pageant wagons, and the display, as a whole, mirrors the unified parade of plays; however, instead of a series of stories, the Mepkin Crèche Festival presents the same story again and again. The viewers must, therefore, focus on each individual scene while contemplating its relationship to the others and how they all coalesce into a single drama. In the end, when they leave the festival, each viewer will have formed not a single interpretation of the Nativity but rather a multilayered understanding of the iconic event and its significance throughout the world.

*Christmas began in the heart of God. It is complete only when it reaches the heart of man.*

ANONYMOUS

$S$omehow,
God took a handful of humanity:
Proud, petulant, passionate;
And a handful of divinity:
Undivided, inexpressible, incomprehensible:
And enclosed them in one small body.

Somehow, the all too human
Touched the divine.
And was not vaporized.
To be human was never the same,
But forever thereafter,
Carried a hint of its close encounter with the perfect.
and forever thereafter,
God was never the same,
But carried a hint of the passion of the mortal.

IAN OLIVER

T*he journey is essential to the dream.*

FRANCIS OF ASSISI

## The Rising Star of the East:
## How We Adore Thee

*As my fingers connected fabric to fabric, forming images of the Nativity, my heart rejoiced and sang: Behold let us adore Him. In my image, the Baby Jesus, wrapped in swaddling clothes, rests in the manger as Joseph and Mary present Him to the world. While engaged in my devotional creative work, the adoration of the Magi and Shepherds seemed to take on a full and present life to me as my fingers sewed them into the fabric of the Stable. I could almost smell and feel their gifts of myrrh, frankincense, and gold. My senses and my heart sang carols of praise: Silent Night, Noel, O Come, O Come, Emmanuel, until at last, I knew that I was no longer the artist creating, but rather the stable itself, revealing the Blessed event of the Rising Star of the East: Come let us adore Him.*

PEGGIE L. HARTWELL
SUMMERVILLE, SOUTH CAROLINA

$T$he way to Christmas
lies through an ancient gate . . .
It is a little gate,
child-high,
child-wide,
and there is a password:
"Peace on earth to
men of good will."
May you, this Christmas,
become as a little child again
and enter into His kingdom.

ANGELO PATRI

. . . So it is almost an abstract, philosophical representation rather than a very tangible, full blown artistic representation. Such diversity means that we are talking about a mystery that is of such diversity that one aspect of it does not define the whole thing. In fact, that's what mystery is. It keeps shining at you and we keep picking up different reflections of something that we really can't look at straight on because it is so rich and bright.

Father Francis Kline, O.C.S.O.
NATIVITY: THE ART AND SPRIRIT OF THE CRÈCHE

*A*dvent is the 'sacrament' of the
presence of God in His world, in the
mystery of Christ at work in History…

THOMAS MERTON

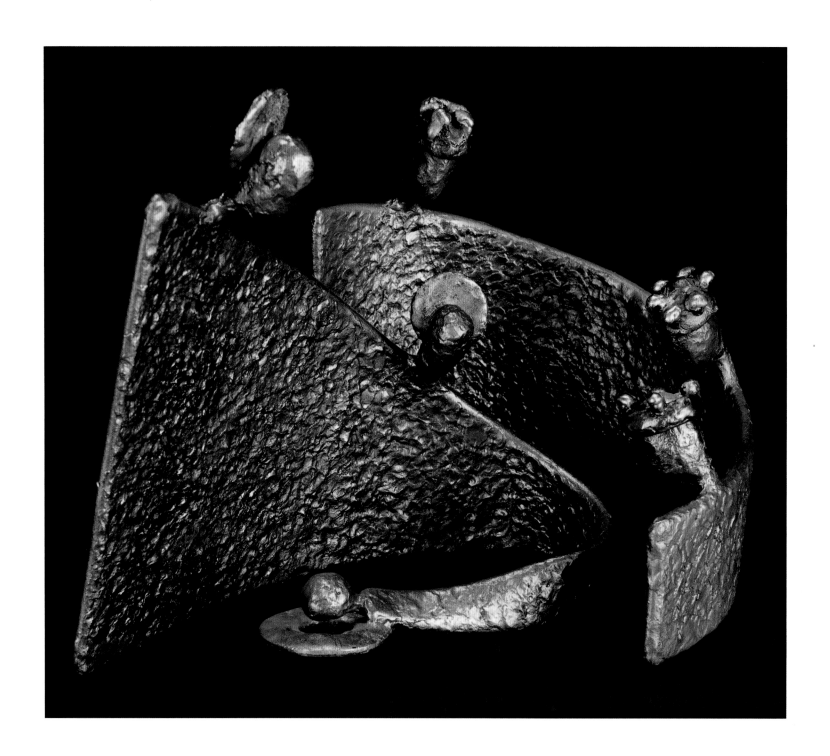

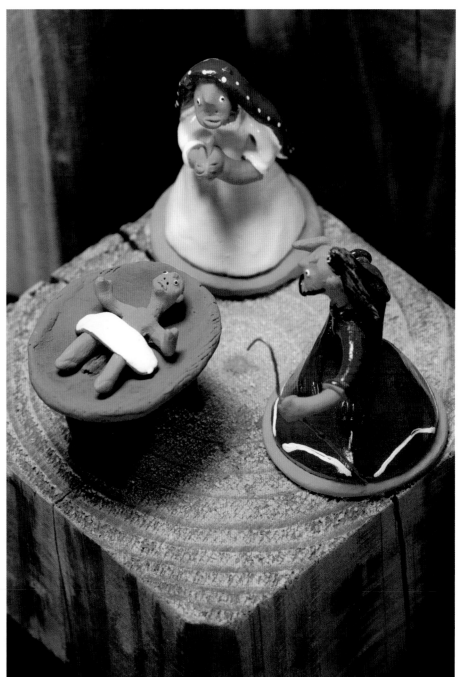

# Night Passage to Bethlehem

*He who keeps you will not slumber.* Psalm 121 vs. 3

I am a quilter and receive great pleasure deciding which colors and fabrics to use in a pieced quilt. Over the years, I have gone from traditional patterns to more contemporary designs. Recently, however, I have become acquainted with the ancient art of felting, a technique used in many cultures around the world, and one that takes advantage of wool's natural tendency to mat together in a thick, textured material.

For this piece, the image of Mary and Joseph walking to Bethlehem on a cold, dark night seems well suited to the rugged, organic appearance of felted wool. I used a combination of techniques to compose the piece, including wet felting, machine needle felting, and hand needle felting. Through my work I have learned that felting is much like painting; rather than using the stroke of a brush to make subtle changes, the artist instead uses a few strands of wool to give shadow, depth, or highlighting.

The image is a poignant one to me: a couple, pregnant with child, trudges alone through a dark wood. And yet the full moon lights their way and conveys a benign, caring presence as surely as the omnipresent God who loves them and watches over them. My intent is for the viewer to identify with this holy couple, and recall that while we may sometimes be lonely, we are never alone.

Carolyn Thiedke, MD
Sullivan's Island, South Carolina

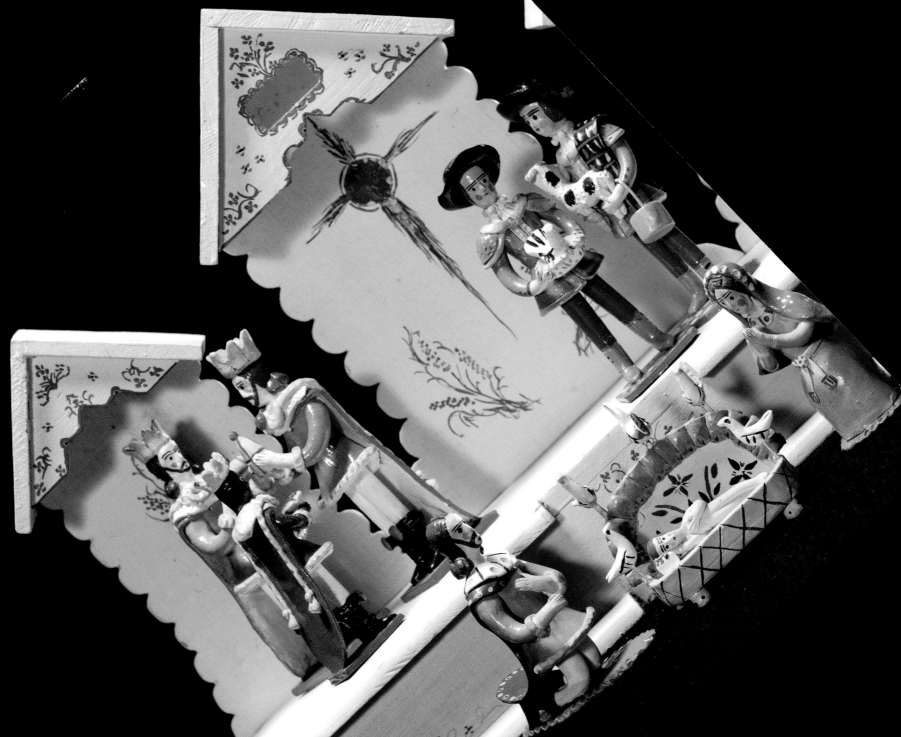

In the last analysis, the best Christmas sermon is preached by the silence of the Divine Infant in the crib. Those who have ears to hear must listen to what 'the loving and mystical silence of the eternal Word says to us.' By the effect of this upon their souls, the saints who contemplate Him are reduced to deep and reverent silence, and in this silence they hear the message which His silence speaks to them: it is the message of peace . . .

THOMAS MERTON
*SERMON THREE*

$A$nd so, brothers, faith working in you through charity has been born of the Holy Spirit. Guard it, nurture it tenderly, as the Infant Christ, until the Child Who was born for you may be formed in you.

THOMAS MERTON
*SERMON FOUR*

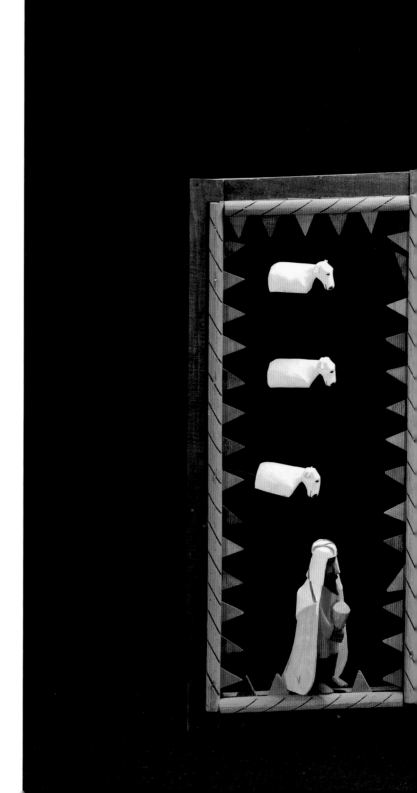

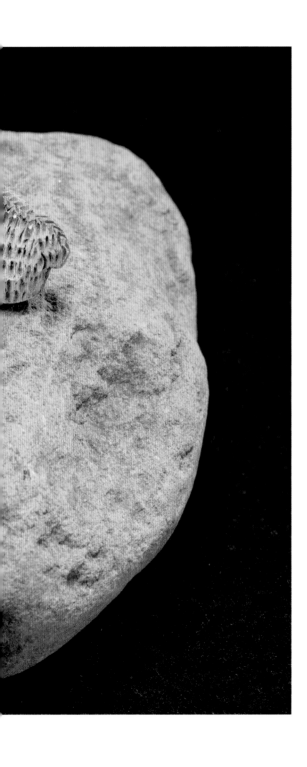

With filial love let us contemplate Christ in the swaddling clothes with which Mary wrapped Him. In everlasting joy let us look upon the glory and beauty in which the Father arrayed Him—glory such as belongs to the Father's Only-begotten Son. To Him with the Father and the Holy Spirit be honor and glory forever.

THOMAS MERTON
*SERMON FIVE*

## Mosaic Crèche

This particular sculpture is a model for what I hope to be a much larger outdoor three-dimensional mosaic crèche. I want the figures to appear as if they are growing from the ground in much the same way as a cypress tree. The figures will connect to the earth as naturally as a tree trunk, leading us upward in much the same way that the miraculous birth of Jesus leads us naturally from this world to the next. The choice to use the medium of mosaic comes from my interest in taking broken, cast-off pieces from different forms and objects and putting them back together to create a unified, harmonious whole. This transformation reminds me of what Jesus sets out to do in our lives—to transform our brokenness into the beautiful men and women we are meant to be.

ANGEL ALLEN
COLUMBIA, SOUTH CAROLINA

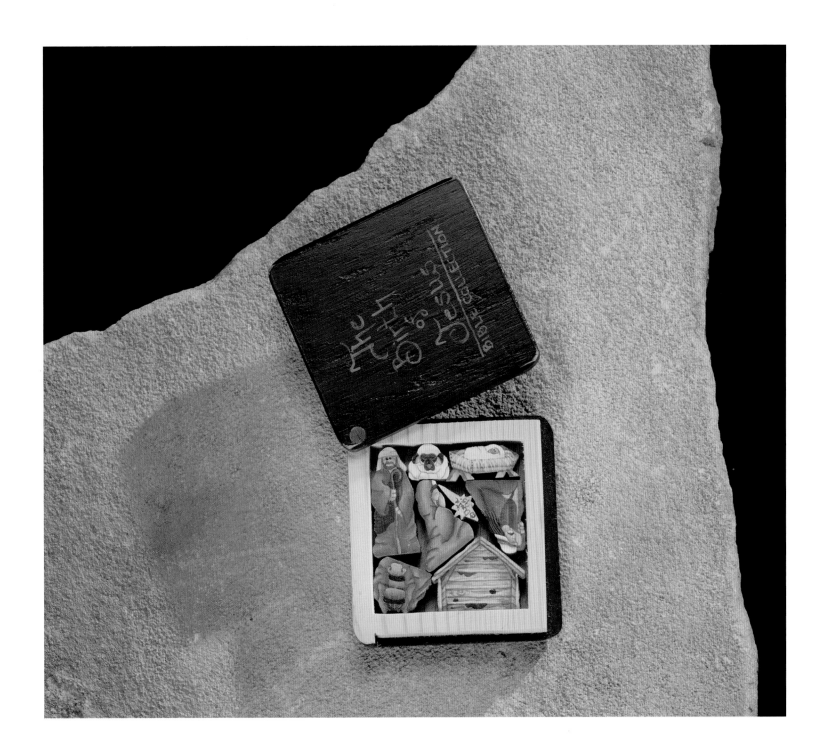

*God grant you the light in Christmas, which is faith;*
*the warmth of Christmas, which is love;*
*the radiance of Christmas, which is purity;*
*the righteousness of Christmas, which is justice;*
*the belief in Christmas, which is truth;*
*the all of Christmas, which is Christ.*

WILDA ENGLISH

$W$hat is Christmas?
*It is tenderness for the past, courage
for the present, hope for the future.
It is a fervent wish that every cup
may overflow with blessings rich
and eternal, and that every path
may lead to peace.*

AGNES M. PHARO

# How Can I Keep From Singing?*

## THE NATIVITY AS IF IT WERE HAPPENING TODAY

This archival print is of a triptych, or three-panel painting. The original is in watercolor, and measures 40" x 90." Archival means that the inks used to print it are designed to last for 200 years, as long as the painting is not hung in bright sunlight. It took 200+ hours to complete.

This painting echoes a long-established concept and tradition. One day I was reviewing a Rembrandt Nativity with a humanities class at Berea College. Though Rembrandt depicted a beloved Christian subject, he placed it in a Dutch barn, with Dutch animals. The setting was Dutch, and the models for all the players in the drama were certainly Dutch. They were

159

depicted as if this all took place in Rembrandt's time, not in biblical time. I asked the college students how Joseph would be dressed if I followed this tradition, and they suggested Levis, a sweatshirt, and running shoes. Each element was considered, with similar results that keyed it undeniably into our era. It's obvious that Michelangelo, Da Vinci, and many others did the same, retelling the Bible stories visually and thereby making them more available to viewers.

An example: In a tiny church in the Tuscan hills of Italy is a primitive wall painting of the Nativity. A bit further along the wall is a window. The artist used the mountain view from the window to place his religious subject. Doing that, he brought it close to the people of this town and time.

Here is a short list of some of the nods given to artistic and historical tradition in my painting. This tradition of many figures and animals is from the Italian Presepio, in which the whole world looks on the special event of the Nativity:

- **The star** *is a galaxy.*
- **Mary and Joseph** *are dressed as 2003 (when the painting was completed) young parents.*
- **Jesus** *looks like a baby, not a wizened little man. Rabbits and a ball that is our earth are his playthings.*
- **The Three Kings or Wise Men** *are an African woman in tribal dress, an American Indian on horseback, and a businessman in a gray flannel suit.*
- **The landscape** *is a view of the mountains surrounding Berea.*
- **The barn** *is a building being built in the country.*
- **A boy playing a trumpet** *"makes a loud noise" unto the Lord.*
- **An Italian peasant** *with a water jug pauses to watch.*
- **A juggler** *uses more balls than humanly possible. One is our earth itself.*
- **Two children attend and bring a gift**. *The boy holds out his favorite stuffed animal.*
- **A jester (Clown of God)**, *a boy, and a farmer watch.*
- **A Native American older woman** *is in her wheelchair.*
- **A rural housewife** *brings a pie she's made, as her husband gently holds her arm.*
- **An angel** *floats above the tableau.*
- **A Chinese AIDS doctor and researcher** *stands in happy awe.*
- **A German boy** *brings a seasonal giant gingerbread cookie to the Infant.*
- **A second jester figure,** *ready to entertain, holds balloons made of colored pig bladders.*
- **A mountain woman,** *arms folded, observes skeptically.*

- **A skateboarder** *soars while taking his place in the event.*
- **The Artist** *stands with brushes in hand and painting apron, while his dog, Gretel, positions herself at his side.*
- **Predatory birds** *in the sky imply future trials and dangers.*
- **A scarecrow**, *right center panel, foreshadows the Crucifixion.*
- **A tiny skull**, *left panel at the feet of the mountain woman, is a "memento mori," which reminds us of the mortality we all share with Christ.*
- **The leopard** *and the lamb lie down together in the central panel as a ewe and newborn lamb reflect on Mary's gentle warmth toward Jesus.*
- **Other animals** *come from the artist's own Kentucky experience.*

NEIL DI TERESA
* FROM THE CHRISTIAN HYMN BY ROBERT WADSWORTH LOWERY

O *Father may that Holy Star*
*Grow every year more bright,*
*And send its glorious beams afar*
*To fill the world with light.*

WILLIAM CULLEN BRYANT

O sweet and sacred childhood,
which brought back humanity's true
innocence, by which persons of every
age can return to blessed childhood
and be conformed to you.

BLESSED GUERRIC OF IGNY
*THE FIRST SERMON FOR CHRISTMAS*

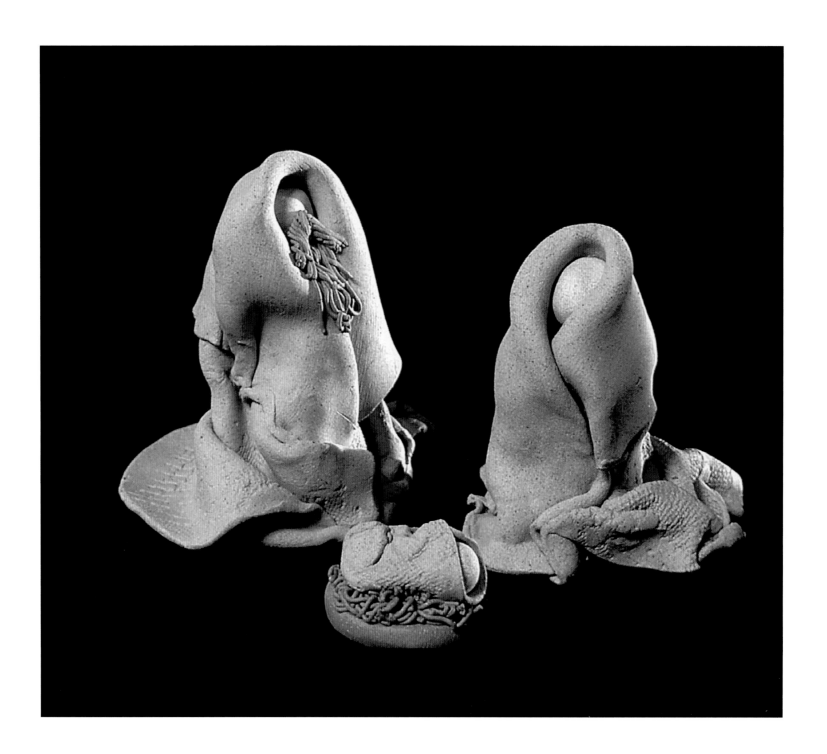

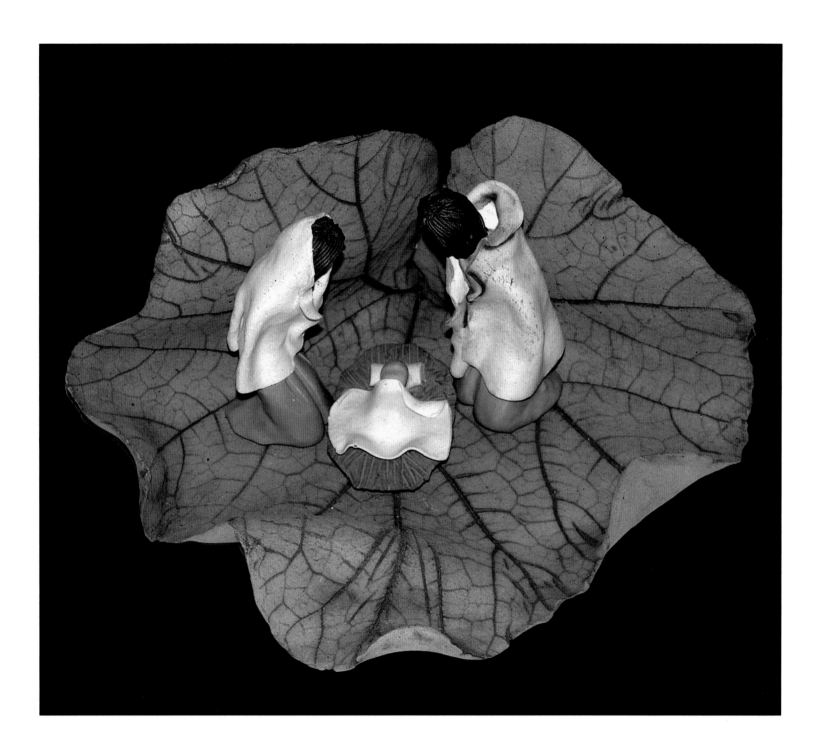

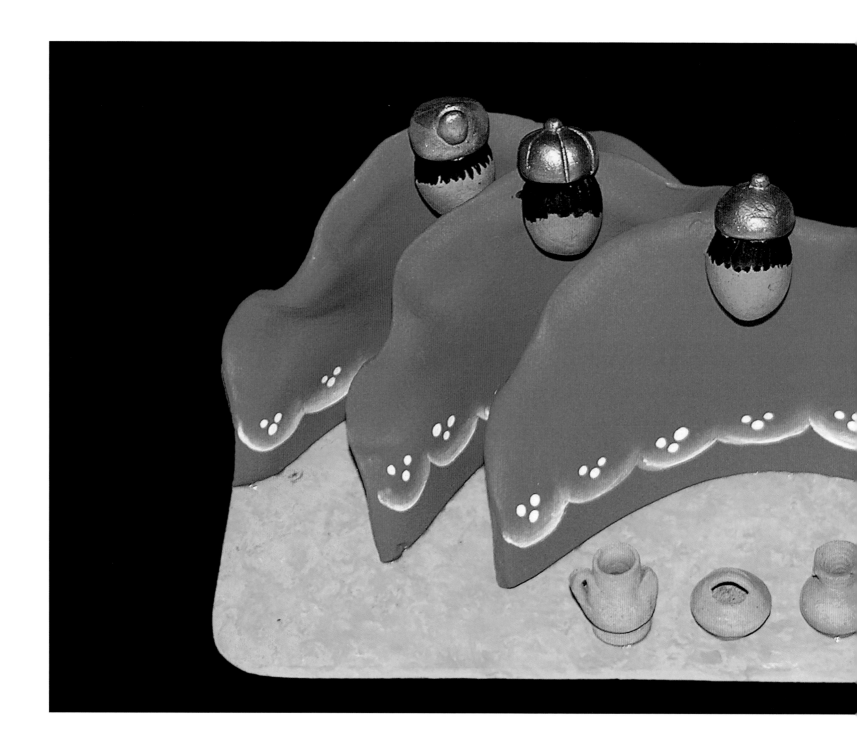

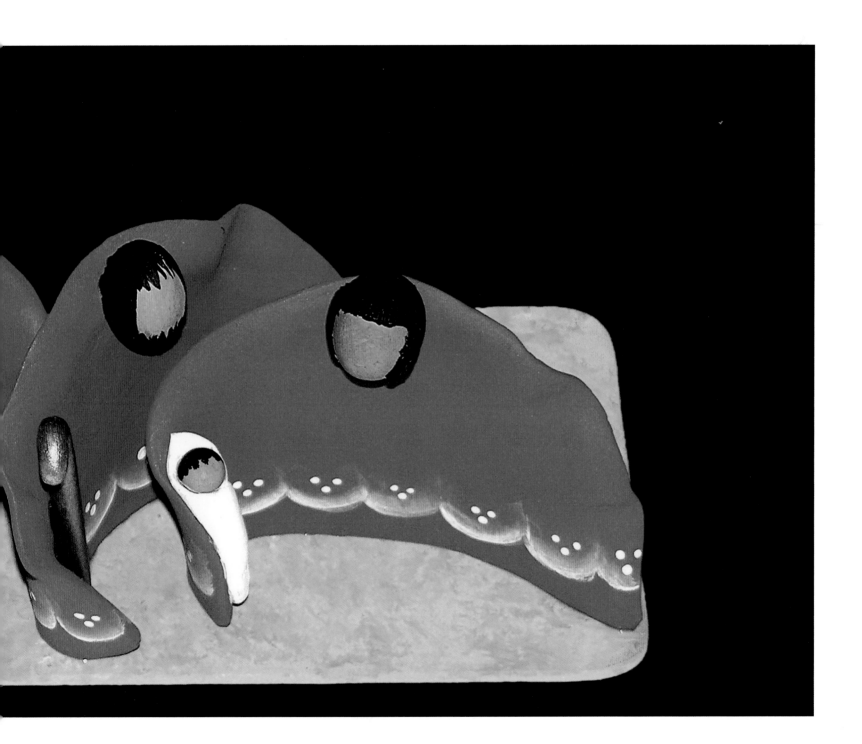

## Jesus and Flock

**M**y initial idea for the shepherd and his flock was to have the shepherd represent the Monk and be surrounded by sheep, all facing the baby Jesus. I use discarded materials in most of my work; here I tried to stay as monochromatic as I could: the rusting of the metal tones with the grays of the concrete contrasts with the gold and silver leaf of the baby Jesus. This year, I am adding Joseph and Mary, and I am intentionally positioning them so their faces are not seen. In the piece we are looking over the shoulder of a shepherd who, along with Joseph and Mary, is looking down at the manger. The sheep are facing the viewer, and as the viewer approaches the manger, they then see the baby Jesus. The materials I used include the following:

Jesus lies in a concrete manger with a faux box finish outside and gold leaf inside. Jesus (along with the other figures) is cut from a gray water tank – all monochromatic except for the area around Him.

Three sheep – all made from a water tank – gaze upon Jesus with eyes made of lightbulbs and wool from old bedsprings.

The kneeling shepherd is made from the water tank and found objects. His staff is the high point – he is seen from the back – as the viewers look over his shoulder.

The bases are all independent of each image, and are secured by bolts embedded in the concrete.

The overall scene is monochromatic, with the gold leaf around the baby Jesus as the focus. The manger is hiding a single light source; the figure of Jesus is covering the light hitting the leafing.

JEFF KOPISH
CHARLESTON, SOUTH CAROLINA

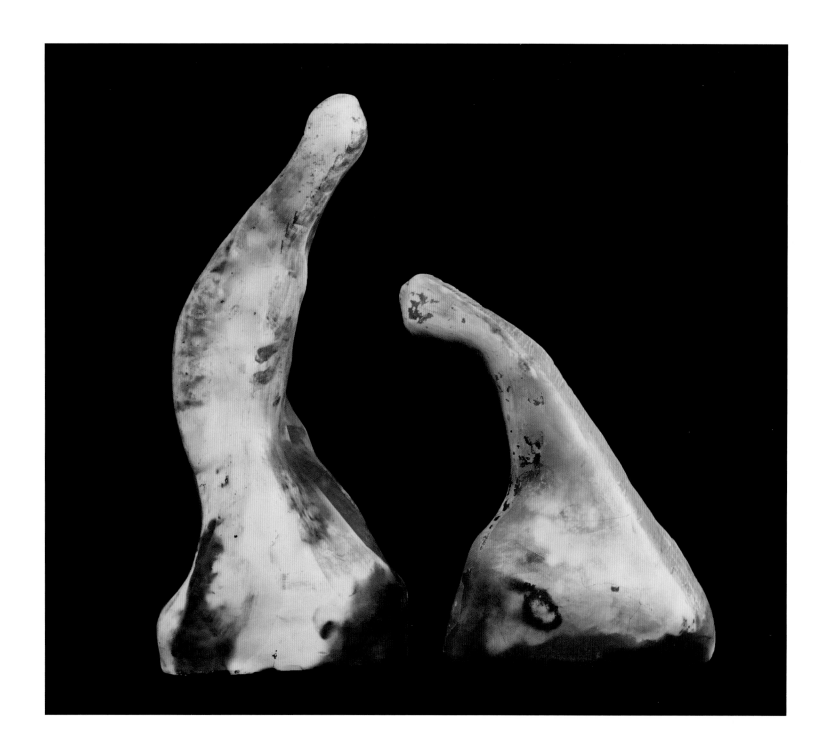

The earth has grown old with its burden of care.
But at Christmas it always is young,
The heart of the jewel burns lustrous and fair.
And its soul full of music breaks the air,
When the song of angels is sung.

PHILLIP BROOKS

# Good News of Great Joy

This piece depicts the angel delivering the message to the shepherds. In this piece I wanted to portray a large, ethereal angel and the words the angel delivered, with the shepherds all framed in this extraordinary experience of receiving the good news. The hillside where the shepherds stand is stamped with images of human figures, which represent the people to whom the shepherds spread the good news of great joy of the Savior being born.

CASSIE RYALLS
ASHEVILLE, NORTH CAROLINA

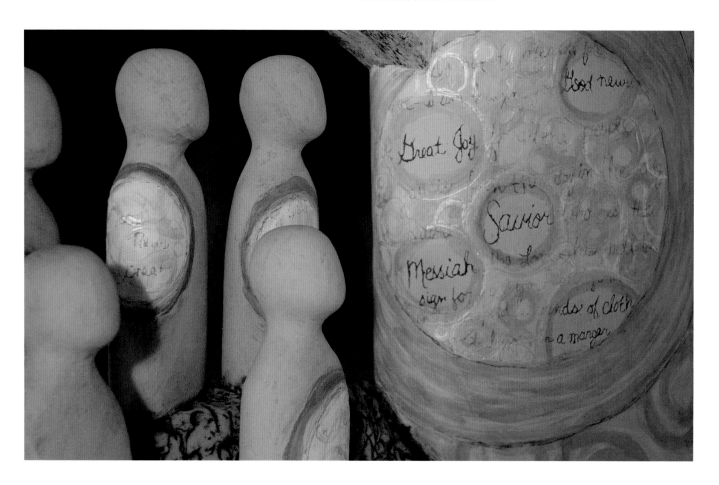

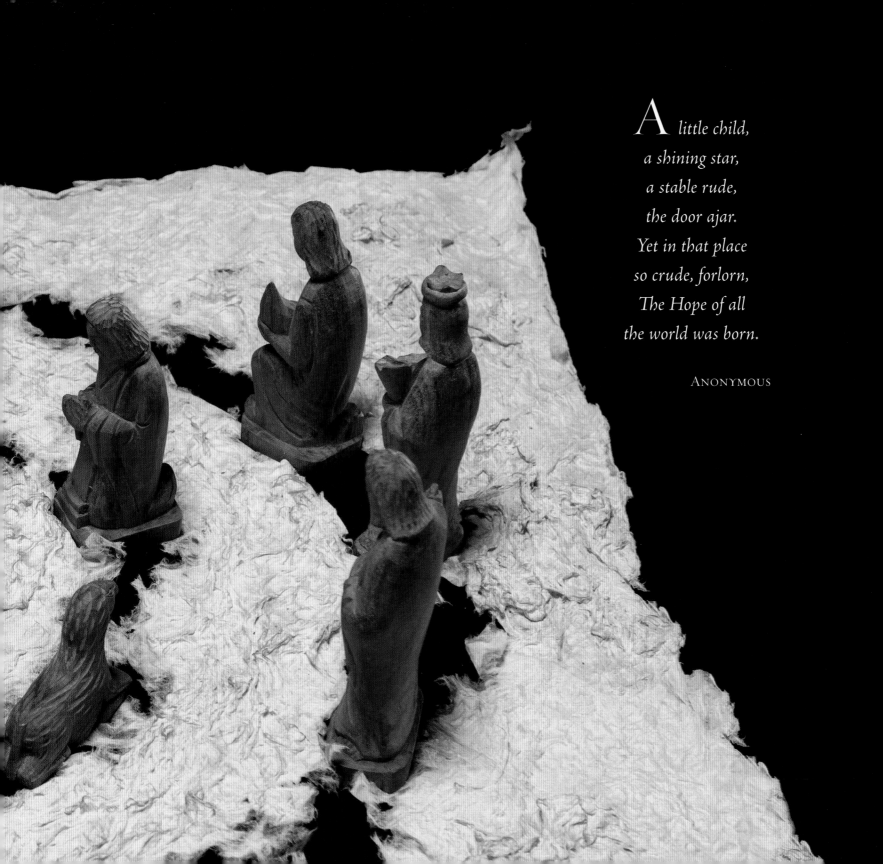

A little child,
a shining star,
a stable rude,
the door ajar.
Yet in that place
so crude, forlorn,
The Hope of all
the world was born.

ANONYMOUS

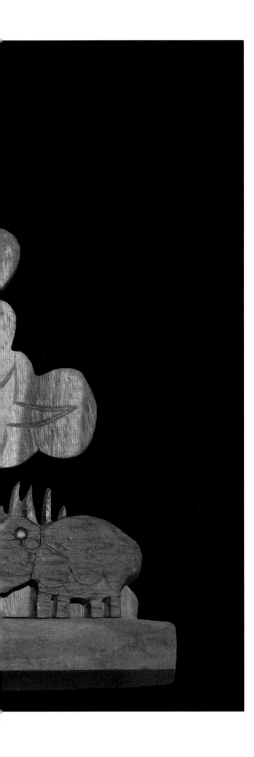

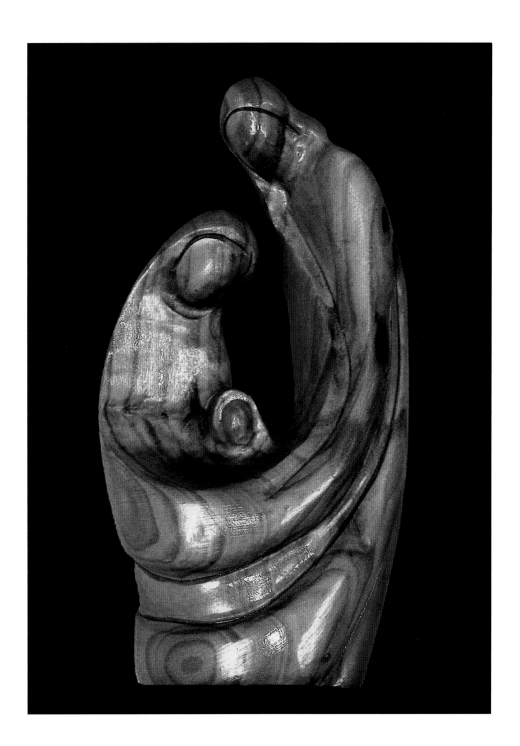

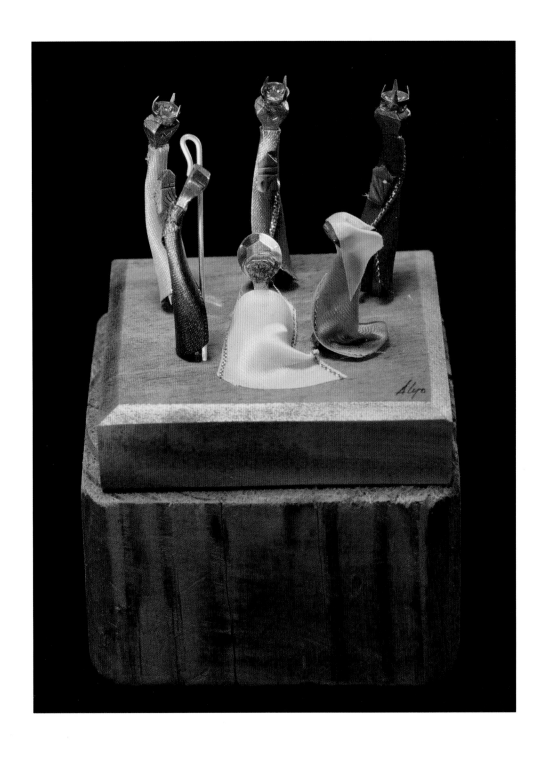

## Soapstone Crèche

This crèche is carved in "Black Pearl" soapstone from Virginia. Soapstone, or steatite, is a very dense, heavy stone, but is also quite soft and easily carved, as it is a massive form of talc. The talc gives it a slippery feeling like soap.

Soapstone is the first stone that I carved as a child and I have used it all my professional life. I love the way it can be worked quickly with hammer and chisel and rasp, and finer details rendered with wood carving tools. It lends itself, as any stone does, to simpler forms, like the carvings of the Inuit people of the North. They have always favored soapstone for their beautiful depictions of their people's activities and the animals they hunt. These have been a great influence on my own work.

Since this soapstone crèche is designed for reproduction, I have kept the forms and the gestures simple but telling.

MARY ELDREDGE
SPRINGFIELD, VERMONT

# APPENDIX

# PATRONS

Richard and LaVonne Abbott
Dr. and Mr. Donald Ahern
Alba Ambert, *in memory of Isabel Oliveras*
Anonymous
Herbert and Sylvia Ayars
Mary L. Ballou, *in memory of Bill Ballou*
George and Eleanor Barna
Katherine C. Battle
Robert H. Becker, *in memory of Robert P. and Rose M. Becker*
Charles Beischel
Charlene Bell
Al and Elaine Bellacicco
Berlin's Restaurant Supply, Inc.
Mr. and Mrs. George B. Bishop, Jr.
Guy and Gail Blanton
Trent and Dori Bolling
Dr. Dan and Sue R. Brake
Mr. and Mrs. Richard J. Brownyard
Nick and Liz Bruno
Dr. Bill and Joyce Burch
Barbara Burgess and John Dinkelspiel
Linda P. Burton
Beth and Larry Burtschy
Jay Butler
Mr. and Mrs. Mark W. Buyck, Jr.
Burt and Nina Carlin *in honor of our sons Drew, Brett, and Paul*
Mr. and Mrs. Wilfred Caron, *in memory of Roland E. Caron*
Laurie M. Carter
Dr. and Mrs. William C. Carter III
Mr. and Mrs. William Cary
Kathleen Cassels, *in memory of Catherine Cassels*
Msgr. Patrick J. Caverly, *in memory of Fr. Francis Kline*
Central True Value
Church of Christ Our King
Church of the Nativity, Utica, Ohio
Helen Clark
Henry J. and Sandra G. Clark
Charles Combier, *in memory of Madeleine Combier*
William and Trudy Cooper, *in memory of Abbott Francis Kline*
Charles and Ginny Crone
Rev. Dr. Karen Bascom Culp
Robert David Cummings, *Happy Birthday Jennifer Stewart*
Jim and Mary Jo Daugherty
Glen Dawn and Catherine Todd
Mr. an Mrs. W. H. deButts, Jr., *in memory of Abbott Francis Kline*
Dr. Danny and Babs DeCamps
Lynda deMarsh-Mathews, *in memory of M. J. Soltow*

Mrs. James D. Decker
Dr. and Mrs. Victor Del Bene
Richard and Lorraine Delmonte
Delta Pharmacy and Medical Supply
Grace B. DeWitte
Mr. and Mrs. A. B. Dodge, *in memory of Father James Dodge*
Walter V. Duane, *in memory of deceased members of Duane Family*
Carol and Kevin Duggan
James Dunlap and Thomas Toner, *in memory of the Dunlap and Toner families*
Eastern Electric Supply, *in memory of Margaret Wells Davis*
William and Patricia Easterlin
Edmund Elder, *in memory of Margaretta Crow*
Richard and Sandy Ferencz
Dr. and Mrs. Richard Fitzgerald
The Gagnon Family
Joan and Lawrence Germano, *in memory of Brother Joseph Lawrence, OCSO*
Roger and Nancy Goedtel
Gina Goff
Richard and Susan Gotheridge
Cely M. Gozum, *in memory of Rogelio T. Gozum*
Mrs. Berkeley Grimball
T. Patrick Halaiko and Catherine Blackford
Katherine Hall
Ann K. Hargett, *in memory of The Reverend William Murray Hargett*
Linda Harkey, *in memory of Louise Eckard Keating*
Rae Hartman, MD
The Heckel Family, *in memory of August and Leah Heckel*
Casey and Sunshine Herbert
Frank and Mary Bonaccorsi Herzel
Karen and Rhoda Hiott, *in memory of Claude and Pearl Hiott*
Nancy D. Holcombe
Hometown Bath and Body
Atticus Humphries
Edward A. Janak, Jr., *in memory of Edward A. Janak*
Dr. Wendell S. Johnson, *in memory of Mary Mixon Johnson*
Paul K. Kania
Linda Kareiva
Joe and Vivian Kaz
Milton and Brenda Kelley
Frank and Betty Anne Kenney, *in memory of Sr. Mary Albert, MSBT*
Helen L. King
Edwin J. Kinney
Fay Klatte, *in honor of Mrs. Shizuko Klatte*
Mark W. Knockemus
H. L. Koester III, *in memory of Dr. Gene E. Burges, M.D., PhD*
Hugh C. Lane, *in memory of Beverly G. Lane*

Mariano La Via, *in memory of the La Via and Faulkner families*
Elizabeth W. Lawson
George Lensing
Emmanuel and Edith Lepoutre
Angela Lindner, *in memory of Ralph and Minerva Stephenson*
Joyce Llleyln, *in memory of Thomas J. Lalley*
Linda Macedo
Tom and Susan Mahan
Pat Marriott
Tommy and Sue Matthews
Dr. and Mrs. Joseph McAlhany, Jr.
Lorraine and Tom McDermott
Arthur W. and Gloria E. McDonald
Harriett McDougal, *in memory of James Oliver Rigney, Jr.*
Fr. Michael J. McNally
Mary E. Mestrez
Rosalie Mir
Martha Ann Monroe
Dr. and Mrs. Richard Leland Morrison III
Bart Mullin
Cal and Maryln Myers
James and Christina Myers
Christina and Jack Nietert
Dick and Wanda Orman
Fr. Frank O'Rourke
Richard and Stephanie Paetsch
Norma and John Palms
Joe and Mack Pazdan
Carlos and Justine Pena, *in memory of Carlos and Margot Pena
and Hattie V. Bishop*
The Family of T. Ashton Phillips, Sr.
Piggly Wiggly Carolina Company
The Pinckneys, *in memory of Millie P. Boykin*
Jan and David Ploth, *in memory of L. Dean Peterson*
Mrs. Robert Preston, *in memory of Dr. Robert A. Preston*
Dr. and Mrs. A. Bert Pruitt
Dora Ann and James Reaves
Dr. and Mrs. Jerry Reves
Francine Reed and Charlotte Crosby
Rev. Charles H. Rhodes
Lila K. and James R. Ridlen
Rose Riordan, *in memory of Josephine Novosel*
Carolyn Rivers and Henk Brandt
Greg and Mary Robinson
Dottie Roddy
Alan and Amy Romanczuk, *in memory of Ruthe G. Nadel*
Father John Peter Rosson
Jim and Kathy Rozier

Mary and Charles Rudloff, *in memory of Robert Stephen "Bobby" Rudloff*
Nicholas and Nancy Rutgers, Jr.
Roland W. and Charlotte Sacks
Mr. and Mrs. John J. Saueracker
Janet Schaaf
Seabrook Island Natural History Group
David J. Shaw
Mr. and Mrs. Joseph P. Short, Jr.
Fr. John Silver, *in memory of Rosemary McGurn Silver*
Sisters of Charity of Our Lady of Mercy
Sisters of Charity of St. Augustine
Charles E. Spigelmire III
St. Benedict Catholic Church Women's Club
Mr. and Mrs. Harold R. Stein
Caroline J. Stoll
Rev. Lawrence R. Strittmatter, *in memory of The Strittmatter and McTighe families*
Frank and Carol Strunk, daughter and granddaughter
Patricia Sturbaum, *in memory of David Sturbaum*
Mr. and Mrs. John G. Sullivan
Hariette and Skip Swearingen
Dr. and Mrs. James D. Taggart
Dr. and Mrs. James D. Taggart, *in memory of Br. Edward Shivell, OCSO*
Jane Talbot, *in memory of Francis F. Talbot*
Jane and Virginia Tezza
Peter Tezza Family
Virginia Tezza, *in memory of Mrs. Camilla Tezza*
Carolyn Thiedke and Fred Thompson
Jane Wilroy Trinkley
Rev. Gerald S. Twomey, *in memory of Eileen Kathryn and
John Arthur Twomey, Sr.*
Jane L. Tyler and Curtis Worthington
Mrs. Cecilia M. Velte, *in memory of Msgr. Richard C. Madden*
Wanda Villeponteaux, *in memory of Jack A. Villeponteaux and David Umphlett*
Dr. and Mrs. L. Dieter Voegele
Al Walker
Mary and Steve Walker
Peter Wallace and Judith Kramer
Todd and Ginger Walter
E. D. Warwick, *in memory of A. J. O'Connell*
Joyce J. Waters
Mary L. Way
Thomas S. Weaver
Beth Williams, *in memory of Fr. Francis Kline*
Willliams Farm Supply
Dr. and Mrs. Jerald Yaden
Mike and Julie Yaeger
Walter and Mary Ziegler

Printed and bound in China through Asia Pacific Offset Inc.

Published by Mepkin Abbey
1098 Mepkin Abbey Road
Moncks Corner, South Carolina 29461

First Edition

ISBN 978-1-934424-01-8

Produced by Lionheart Books, Ltd.
3522 Ashford Dunwoody Road, #229
Atlanta, Georgia 30319

Designed by Michael Reagan

Pages 4, 6 & 7 © Katherine L. Hare, Pages 16, 17, 18, 20, 21, 22 & 23 © John McWilliams; Pages 42 & 43 © Angel Allen;
Pages 47, 50 & 120 © Rick Rhodes; Pages 11, 24, 29, 52 & 53 © Timothy Reagan; Page 74 © Michael Reagan; Page 174 © Stephen Feryus;
Pages 158, 159 & 161 © Neil di Teresa; Pages 180, 181 © Evan Wathen; Pages 54, 57, 167, 168, 169,175, 185 © Pat Marriott;
Pages 19, 37, 41, 46, 51, 75, 76, 78, 79, 80, 166, 184, 187 & 189 from the Mepkin Abbey Collection.

## Acknowledgments

To the Mepkin Abbey Store Board who inspired the Crèche Festival when Arthur McDonald said "I'll do the staging," Judith Kramer said
"I'll design the path," Celia Cerasoli said "I'll do the flyer and program," Barbara Burgess said "I'll coordinate the volunteers," Al Walker said,
"I'll lend you some of my best sets," and Peggy Savlo said "I'll introduce you to my friend and crèche collector, Earl Kage," our most heartfelt thanks.

And our deepest appreciation to those Committee Chairs who coordinate the generous service of the dedicated volunteers who
make the festival such an experience of community: Michael Yaeger – Trees, Julie Yaeger and Fran Taggart – Volunteers,
Donald Pefferkorn –Transportation, Jamie Nelson – Wreath, Francie Humphrey – Casting Crew, and Fr. Guerric,
Arthur McDonald, Judith Kramer, Mary Walker and Jeff Kopish – Selection and Event Coordination.

Finally, a special thank-you to Lisa and Michael Reagan from Lionheart Books who called forth the book,
David Edwards who did the photography (unless otherwise indicated), Martha Peeples Attisano, Editor,
and the hundreds of patrons who have helped make the book more available.